Poverty and Social Justice

Critical Perspectives

Bilingual Press/Editorial Bilingüe

General Editor
Gary D. Keller

Managing Editor
Karen S. Van Hooft

Senior Editor
Mary M. Keller

Assistant Editor
David C. Rubí D.

Address
Bilingual Review/Press
Hispanic Research Center
Arizona State University
Tempe, Arizona 85287
(602) 965-3867

Poverty and Social Justice

Critical Perspectives

A Pilgrimage Toward
Our Own Humanity

Edited by
Francisco Jiménez

Bilingual Press/Editorial Bilingüe
TEMPE, ARIZONA

ISBN: 0-916950-75-1
Printed simultaneously in a softcover edition. ISBN: 0-916950-76-X

Library of Congress Catalog Card Number: 87-70500

PRINTED IN THE UNITED STATES OF AMERICA

Cover photo, "My Hands, Death Valley," © Judy Dater, 1980

Cover design by Antonio Zapata

TABLE OF CONTENTS

Acknowledgments   7

Introduction   9

I. Economic and Societal Perspectives

MANUEL VELASQUEZ, Poverty in America   13

MICHAEL HARRINGTON, Causes and Effects of Pov-
erty and Possible Solutions   27

KENNETH ARROW, Redistribution to the Poor: A
Collective Expression of Individual Altruism   39

II. Political Perspectives

JULIAN BOND, Politics and Poverty   47

CESAR CHAVEZ, Poverty and the Plight of the Farm
Worker   57

SHARON N. SKOG, Reaganomics, Women and
Poverty   63

III. Philosophical and Cultural Perspectives

FRANCES MOORE LAPPE, The Myths About Poverty
and Hunger in America   77

ONORA O'NEILL, Rights, Obligations and World
Hunger   86

PAUL STEIDL-MEIER, S.J., Is Poverty an Injustice?   101

IV. Theological and Religious Perspectives

WILLIAM WOOD, S.J., An Affluent American Re-
sponding to Global Poverty   115

ROBERT MCAFEE BROWN, Poverty and Conscience   127

FRANCIS R. SMITH, S.J., The Catholic Church and
the Poor   139

Contributors   149

Selected Bibliography   155

ACKNOWLEDGMENTS

I wish to acknowledge my debt to my colleagues and friends at Santa Clara University who assisted me with the Institute on Poverty and Conscience and with the preparation of this work. I wish to thank Mario Belotti, Charles E. French, Alma M. García, Rev. Daniel Germann, S.J., Matt Meier, Rev. Charles Phipps, S.J., Philip Boo Riley and Teresa Torres for serving on the Institute Planning Committee; Rev. William J. Rewak, S.J., President of Santa Clara University, for sponsoring the Institute; Rev. Paul Locatelli, S.J., Academic Vice President, and Don Dodson, Associate Academic Vice President, for their support and encouragement. In addition, special thanks to Christine Long and Peg Major for helping me with some of the editing, and to Celeste Fritchle whose secretarial assistance was invaluable and whose advice constantly helped me to see what I had not seen before.

I would like to thank Santa Clara University for granting a Presidential Research Grant to undertake this task. I also want to express my debt to my colleague and friend Philip Boo Riley who was responsible for writing the grant proposal, and who helped me get started on this project.

This book is dedicated to my mother, Joaquina,
whose hands bear the scars of poverty
but whose heart does not.

INTRODUCTION

Like most of the kids he grew up with in Barberton, Ohio—a gritty industrial city south of Akron—Ed Schtucka never expected to be poor.

But soon after he broke his leg at a family reunion, Schtucka was laid off from his $1,490-a-month foreman's job at the Bearfoot Sole shoe plant. Then the plant closed its doors for good—and for the first time the 32-year old father of three found himself needing help.

The family, unable to get welfare or unemployment benefits, scraped by on bags of free groceries from the city-run Barberton Food Pantry and his wife's $442-a-month salary—just $12 more than the couple's monthly mortgage payment.[1]

The Schtuckas are typical of millions of Americans who are experiencing poverty in the 1980s. They are the so-called "new poor"—married couples with children, working families, workers displaced by technological advancement, farmers driven off their lands—who have fallen below the poverty line in large numbers for the first time in recent history.

Stories such as this have appeared in newspapers across the country, providing us with some of the most moving coverage of poverty not only in this country of affluence, but also in other parts of the world. The news media have come into our comfortable living rooms via television and have graphically depicted the effects of poverty in Ethiopia. These pictures of death and suffering engulfing thousands of Ethiopians have taken poverty out of the realm of abstractions and have personalized it. We feel compelled to respond to the misery we see. But we are often overwhelmed and frustrated by the enormity of the problem. For as Michael Harrington states, "it is precisely because poverty has become so much more complex and obdurate, because so many Americans cannot afford to respond to what is seen for them by the media, that such journalism, important as it is, is not enough. There must be much more analysis now."[2]

Poverty and Social Justice: Critical Perspectives (A Pilgrimage Toward

Our Own Humanity) provides such an analysis. The essays included in this anthology are revisions of formal presentations made at Santa Clara University's Institute on Poverty and Conscience.[3] This collection of critical essays has two objectives: first, to encourage readers to increase their awareness and understanding of the origins and nature of poverty as well as possible remedies; second, to challenge them to confront and reflect upon the moral, philosophical and religious dimensions of poverty in our day.

This book is built around four intellectual perspectives: economic, political, philosophical and theological. Each one of these corresponds to one of the four sections into which the anthology is divided. In the first section, "Economic and Societal Perspectives," three different analyses of poverty in contemporary society are presented. Manuel Velásquez provides an overview of poverty in the United States, arguing with statistical data that economic growth alone can not eliminate poverty, and that federal programs to aid the poor make a difference. Michael Harrington explores the dynamics of the "new" poverty in this country and its causes. He offers concrete suggestions for changing the structures in United States and world economies as possible solutions. Kenneth Arrow answers the question: what justification do we have for a government policy of redistribution—a program which would tax the well-off and transfer payments to the worse off? In section two, "Political Perspectives," Julian Bond draws from his extensive political experience to argue that the War on Poverty helped to alleviate poverty in the 1960s, and calls for the revival of a non-partisan national coalition of conscience to carry out the ideals of the Great Society and the New Frontier. César Chávez, founder of the United Farm Workers of America, describes the plight of farm workers, and the successful efforts of the UFW on their behalf. Sharon Skog concludes this section with her essay "Reaganomics, Women and Poverty" in which she assesses Reaganomics and its effects on poor women and children. She offers ten recommendations to help eliminate poverty afflicting women. In the third section, "Philosophical and Cultural Perspectives," the reader is challenged to examine various common assumptions about poverty. Frances Moore Lappé refutes the notion that poverty is inevitable, and invites us to re-examine our most deeply held values in order to create a society worthy of our democratic heritage. Onora O'Neill investigates theories of modern thought on rights and obligations regarding poverty. Similarly, Paul Steidl-Meier discusses the meaning of poverty and the notion of justice. He argues that injustice is found not only in the causes of poverty but also in the fact that no effective political will has developed to overcome it. In the final section, "Theological and Religious Perspectives," the authors draw primarily on the Christian tradition to explore the nature of religious responses to poverty. William Wood points out that American society is afflicted with what he terms the ideology of affluence. This ideology which permeates the economic and social structures of our society contributes to global poverty. He urges us to remove obstacles that prevent the poor from taking charge of their own destiny and to rid ourselves of the ideology of affluence which he believes is destroying us. In his essay "Poverty and Conscience" Robert McAfee Brown defines conscience as it relates to poverty, and discusses the role that the Church should play in dealing with the poor. Frances Smith's essay, "The Catholic Church and the Poor," provides us with a context with which to understand the commitment made to the poor by the Catholic Church in Latin America, and the debate surrounding that pledge.

These twelve essays written by well-known economists, politicians, theologians and philosophers provide us with an interdisciplinary view of poverty. This multi-faceted approach was deemed necessary, for poverty is a multidimensional problem. For example, economic and political decisions are not divorced of philosophical or theological considerations. Policy decisions that affect the welfare of members of society are philosophically grounded. Therefore, to understand current economic policies, we must understand the philosophical or theological foundations upon which these decisions are made.

Besides offering an interdisciplinary approach to the study of poverty, this anthology is unique in two other ways. First, this collection of essays is, for the most part, progressive in point of view. There are several fine works on poverty that present other perspectives. My intent was not to duplicate these, but to offer a comprehensive liberal analysis to the current debate on the most dynamic and vital issue of our time. Second, some of the contributors have experienced poverty firsthand, and have devoted much of their lives—be they political or educational—to the cause of eliminating poverty and injustice. It is not surprising then that their arguments are not only logical in formulation, but also passionate in delivery. Furthermore, even though the authors of these essays discuss poverty from different disciplinary perspectives, they share a common vision: that through our collective efforts poverty can be eliminated. This anthology is an invitation to share in that vision and to make it a reality by joining in that arduous pilgrimage for social justice that might—only might—lead us to our own humanity.[4]

FRANCISCO JIMÉNEZ
SANTA CLARA UNIVERSITY

Notes

[1]"Poor in the U.S.A.", *San Jose Mercury News*, 26 January, 1986, p. 1 and 14A.

[2]*The New American Poverty* (New York: Holt, Rinehart and Winston, 1984), p. 6. Emphasis mine.

[3]This Institute took place during the Winter Quarter of 1985. It consisted of an extensive program of speakers, courses, workshops, films, and conferences. A major highlight of the Institute was a University sponsored conference on the first draft of the American Bishops' Pastoral Letter on "Catholic Social Teaching and the U.S. Economy." The final draft was overwhelmingly approved by the American Bishops at their November 1986 meeting in Washington D.C.

[4]I borrowed this phrase from Michael Harrington's *New American Poverty*, p. 12.

I. Economic and Societal Perspectives

POVERTY IN AMERICA

Manuel Velásquez

It is unfortunate that so many of us know little about the poor who live among us. Sadly, few of us are aware of how many poor there are in the United States, of how fast their numbers have grown, or of how desperate their plight is. To make matters worse, we tend to fill the vacuum of our ignorance by uncritically accepting ideological views about the poor. In spite of easily available evidence to the contrary, we tend to believe that there is much less poverty today than there was, say, twenty years ago; we tend to believe that the poor are "lazy" and "unmotivated"; we uncritically accept the view that "welfare doesn't work"; and we agree that the welfare roles are laden with "welfare cheats." Yet all of these assumptions about the poor are mistaken.

How many poor are there in the United States today? Using the official definition of poverty adopted by the government (which we will examine more closely below) there are today more people in poverty than there were in 1965, the year many of the 1964 "poverty programs" started to take effect. In 1965 there were 33.2 million people below the poverty line. Today there are 35.2 million Americans in poverty. Thus, we have about 2 million more poor people today than we did in 1965 when the so-called "war on poverty" began.[1]

All this does not mean, however, that the number of poor has been continually increasing since 1965. On the contrary, as Table 1 indicates, the number of poor people in this country continued an almost consistent decline between 1965 and the beginning of 1979. By the end of 1978 the number of poor people in America had been reduced to 24.7 million, a reduction of about 9 million human beings from 1965 levels. It is only since 1979 that poverty has been expanding, and it has done so at a terrific pace. In fact, the number of people in poverty increased during the last four years by about the same number of people (9 million) by which it had been reduced during the previous 14 years. In the last four years we have managed to undo the progress of the previous 14.

The reduction of poverty during the 1965-1978 period, and its increase from 1979 to the present, are not due to changes in the size of the population. As Table 1 also indicates, the percent of the population in poverty also decreased during the 1965-1978 period, and it has been increasing from 1979 to the present. The poverty rate decreased from 17 percent in 1965 to 11.4 percent in 1978. Since 1979 it has increased from 11.4 percent to the current 15.2 percent.

TABLE 1

Poverty in the United States

Year	Millions of Poor	% of Population
1965	33.2	17
1970	25.4	13
1975	25.9	12
1978	24.7	11.4
1979	26.1	11.7
1980	29.3	13
1981	31.8	14
1982	34.4	15
1983	35.3	15.2

Defining the Poor

As noted, the figures above are based on the government's official definition of poverty. What is this definition and what does it tell us about the people we count among the poor? The official definition of poverty was developed in 1965 by Mollie Orshansky, a social scientist.[2] Her definition is based on an earlier 1955 government study which reported that poor people tended to spend about a third of their incomes on food. Mollie Orshansky reasoned that since poor people spend about a third of their income on food, we can calculate the income of a poor person if we first know how much a poor person would have to spend on food. It happened that there was another study in 1965 put out by the National Research Council which said that in the United States a family of four could stay alive if they spent at least $2.94 per day on food or about $1073 per year. So Mollie multiplied this figure by three and decided that this was the definition of a poor person: a poor person is one who makes less than three times the minimum amount needed to buy the food to keep that person in reasonable health. In 1965, therefore, a family of four was considered to be in poverty if its income was less than $3,220; because of inflation, the equivalent figure for 1983 was about $10,000. A family of four is considered poor today if its income is less than this amount.

A poverty income is not, of course, a great deal of money. In 1983, for example, a family of four with a poverty income (the bulk of the poor fall far below this income level) had $3,330 to spend on food (i.e., one third of their income). This meant they could spend the magnificent sum of 75 cents per meal per person. The family could spend $3,330 on rent. This meant they had to find a place large enough to house four people at less than $275 per month. (Rents here in the Santa Clara Valley this year [1986] averaged well above $500 for a one-bedroom apartment.) The family then had $3,330 to spend on everything else. This meant each person had about $65 per month to spend on clothes, furniture, bus fare, doctor bills, medicines, light bills, income taxes, movies, and everything else.

There is a major defect in the official government definition of poverty. The official definition takes into account only the money income of the poor: that is, a poor person is one whose total monetary income is below the poverty level. But many of the poor receive in addition to their monetary income, several non-monetary "in-kind" benefits from the government, such as food stamps, Medicaid, and government housing. If the value of the in-kind benefits poor people receive is added to the monetary income they receive, it will turn out that the total net income of many "poor" people is actually above the poverty level. Thus, by failing to include non-cash in-kind benefits in the incomes of the poor, the government counts many more people as falling below the poverty line than actually do.[3]

This defect in the official definition has led some people to draw the perverse conclusion that actually there is almost no poverty in the United States today. They point out that if the total (market) value of all in-kind benefits received by the poor are counted as part of their incomes, then only eight percent to nine percent of the population was poor in 1982.

The major fallacy in this odd argument is that the largest portion of the in-kind benefits received by the poor consists of the very expensive medical care that many elderly poor receive when they are suffering from life-threatening illnesses. An expensive and lengthy stay in the hospital because of pneumonia, for example, may cost, say, $3,000. If an elderly person is $2,000 dollars below the poverty line, his pneumonia will suddenly lift him "above" the poverty line if the value of his stay in the hospital is counted as part of his "income." In reality, however, that poor person is worse off than he was before he received this in-kind "benefit"! Thus, the odd argument that poverty is almost non-existent because the in-kind benefits the poor receive lift most of them above poverty, is nonsense.

Nevertheless, a case can be made that certain benefits the poor receive, such as food-stamps and housing, can legitimately be counted as part of their net income when determining how many people have incomes below the poverty level. In 1979, for example, if money income plus food and housing were counted among the income of the poor, then instead of 26 million poor, there would have been "only" about 22 million poor. In general, counting food and housing benefits as income lowers the official count of the poor by about 15 percent.

However, whereas the official government figures (which count only money income) show that poverty increased by 28 percent between 1979 and 1982, an adjusted definition of poverty that takes into account the in-kind benefits received by the poor would show that poverty increased by an incredible 47 percent between 1979 and 1982.[4] This incredible increase, of course, is due to the fact that funding of in-kind benefits has been declining. Consequently, conservatives today no longer tend to stress the need to count "in-kind" benefits as part of the income of the poor. Taking these "in-kind" benefits into account reveals that the plight of the poor is getting much worse much faster than the "official" poverty figures indicate.

But there are other ways of defining poverty. Definitions of poverty are usually categorized as "absolute" definitions or as "relative" definitions. An "absolute" definition is one which—like the government's official definition—defines a poor person as a person who has less than a certain fixed ("absolute") income or less than a certain fixed level of goods. A "relative" definition is one which defines a poor person as one who has less than a certain proportion of what others in society have.

One influential "relative" definition of poverty is to count as poor all persons whose incomes are among the incomes earned by the poorest 20 percent of the population. In 1983 this would have meant that about 11.6 million families were in poverty. By itself, this bit of information does not tell us very much. However, some interesting facts emerge if we examine the incomes of the poorest 20 percent of the population during the last several years and compare these incomes to those of the rest of the population.

If we examine the Census Bureau's statistics for the last 20 years, then, as Table 2 indicates, there has been very little change in the percent of income that goes to the people in each "quintile" (i.e., in each 20 percent) of the population, at least in the two decades between 1960 and 1979. However, in the four years since 1979 there has been a disturbing change in the incomes going to the various quintiles of the population. During the last four years the three poorest quintiles of the population have lost income, while the two richest quintiles have gained. And these losses and gains are greater than they have ever been in any comparable four-year period in modern history.

TABLE 2

Distribution of Income in the United States

Year	Poorest 20%	Second 20%	Middle 20%	Fourth 20%	Richest 20%
1960	4.8	12.2	17.8	24.0	41.3
1965	5.2	12.2	17.8	23.9	40.9
1970	5.4	12.2	17.6	23.8	40.9
1975	5.4	11.8	17.6	24.1	41.0
1979	5.3	11.6	17.5	24.1	41.6
1983	4.7	11.1	17.1	24.4	42.7

This suggests that during the last four years the poorest 60 percent of the American population has been left worst off, while the richest 40 percent is much better off: what the poor have lost, the rich have gained. This impression is reinforced by the fact that during the last four years the average American is actually poorer than he or she was four years ago. In 1978 and 1979 the median family income (in constant 1982 dollars) was $26,100; at the end of 1983 the median family income was down to $23,793 (also in constant 1982 dollars). Thus, in real terms, the income of the average American family has declined by about $2,300 during the last four years. This decline has been absorbed largely by the poor.

Characteristics of the Poor

It is a common belief that the poor are poor because they do not work. To some extent, this is true. The bulk of the poor do not work. They do not work because they cannot work. In part they cannot work because over half of them are children or elderly. In 1983 12.6 million of the poor were under 16 years of age; 13.8 million were under 18. In 1983, therefore, about 40 percent of the poor were children under 18. In that same year 3.7 million—or 10 percent—of the poor were over 65 years old. Thus, about 50 percent of the poor are either children who are too young to work or elderly who are too old to do so. In addition, 2.9 million (8 percent) of the poor are ill or disabled, and 4.5 million (12 percent) are single parents (80 percent of whom are women) who must stay home to care for their children. Thus, about 70 percent of the poor cannot work because they are children, or elderly, or disabled, or must care for their children. Of the remainder, 9.4 million (27 percent) of the poor worked during 1983.[5]

The poor include disproportionate numbers of minorities and women. In 1983 the poverty rate among blacks was 36 percent, three times the poverty rate among whites (12 percent). The same year the poverty rate of Spanish origin minorities was 28.4 percent, more than twice that of whites. The poverty rate among females was 26 percent in 1983, while among males it was 18 percent. Families headed by women have a poverty rate of 36 percent, three times the rate for all other families (12 percent). In the Bay Area families headed by women constitute 58.6 percent of the Bay Area's poor.[6] Thus race and sex play a strong role in determining who is poor.

Geography also plays a large role in determining who is poor. There are about twice as many poor today in the South (13.5 million) as there are in each of the other three quadrants of the nation (6.6 million in the Northeast; 8.5 million in the Midwest; 6.7 million in the West). The poverty rate is about 18 percent in the South and 13 percent to 14 percent in the rest of the country. The poor are also predominantly trapped in the inner city. The poverty rate in central city areas was about 20 percent in 1983; it was about nine percent in suburban areas.

But the most tragic fact concerning the poor is that, as we have already mentioned, so many of them are children.[7] Between 1979 and 1982 the number of poor children grew by more than 30 percent: from 10 million to 13.3 million. Today, one in five children is poor; one in every four children under the age of six is poor. In California about 1 million children are poor; this means that one in six children in California is poor. In the Bay Area one in nine children is poor. Fifty percent of all black children are poor. Thirty percent of all Hispanic children are poor.

Do Government Programs Help the Poor?

It is often argued, with discouragingly poor logic, that government programs clearly do not help the poor. The argument goes something like this: since the 1964 "War on Poverty" the government has spent disproportionately large amounts of money on programs designed to eradicate poverty. Yet today we have the same high proportion of people in poverty that we did back in 1964. Therefore, government programs have clearly not helped people get out of poverty.

This argument, and others similar to it, are replete with falsehoods and logical fallacies. First, it is false that government programs have had no effect on poverty. As we have already seen, poverty has been declining since the early sixties. In fact, between 1965 and 1978, the poverty rate gradually diminished from 17.3 percent to 11.4 percent. It is only during the last four years, as government programs have been slashed, that poverty has once again begun to rise to those early levels. Secondly, it is a simple logical mistake to argue that because the same proportion of people are in poverty today as several years ago, it must follow that the same people are in poverty today as several years ago. In fact, although the proportion of people in poverty remains fairly constant from year to year, nevertheless, the same individuals do not remain in poverty from year to year because government programs help them emerge from poverty. Individuals fall into poverty because of a variety of unavoidable "crises" such as the death of a spouse, divorce, physical disability, loss of a job, or the birth of children.[8] When they fall into poverty, government programs (which we will examine more closely below) enable them to survive the crisis and get back on their feet. When they are back on their feet, they emerge from poverty. A 1981 University of Michigan study of 12,000 American families discovered that in the course of a decade, a full *25 percent of the American population* will fall into poverty and will receive welfare for a period; but 50 percent will emerge from poverty after less than 20 months; 70 percent will emerge after less than three years; only eight percent will remain in poverty throughout the entire decade.[9]

Thus government programs in reality do help the poor get out of poverty: every year they successfully put millions of poor individuals back on their feet and allow them to permanently climb out of poverty. The proportions of people in poverty do not change rapidly from one year to the next, however, because new people keep falling into poverty as a result of being subjected to the same "crises" that struck a similar proportion of people the year before: death, loss of a job, divorce, childbirth, and so on. But it is a perversion of logic to argue that since these proportions remain fairly constant, it must follow that government programs do not help the poor emerge from poverty. (It is also bizarre to hear people claim that poverty can be eliminated by "improving the economy" as if economic improvements will eliminate death, divorce, disability, childbirth, and the other temporary crises that periodically drop people into poverty.)

Thirdly, it is false that we have spent fantastically large amounts of money on government programs that could eradicate poverty. If we count all of the government funds that end up in the hands of the poor (including not only need-based programs, but also entitlement funds that make their way into the hands of the poor), only about 10 percent of the government's budget is allocated to the poor.

Moreover, the bulk of these government funds are NOT intended to eradicate the CAUSES of poverty: they are merely intended to provide the poor with enough money, food, and medical care to tide them over their hard times. Programs such as President Johnson's Economic Opportunity Act of 1964, which was the heart of his so-called "War on Poverty" and which was aimed at dealing with the CAUSES of poverty, have never been fully funded.[10] The Economic Opportunity Act was supposed to create investment funds as well as jobs and training programs for the poor, but it unfortunately was side-tracked by the Vietnam war. During the years it was in operation, the Economic Opportunity Act was allocated only a fraction of the money that studies had shown would be needed. The same may be said for several other much less ambitious programs that were supposed to deal with the CAUSES of poverty.

Thus, the amount of money that we spend on the poor is relatively little. And what little money we do spend is not aimed at eradicating poverty by getting rid of the CAUSES of poverty: it is merely intended to tide the poor over hard times. So it is perverse to argue that we have spent large sums of money on programs that were supposed to get rid of poverty but which failed.

Welfare Programs and the Poor

Although "welfare" is often criticized, many of us are not aware of exactly what "welfare" programs the United States actually has and how much is spent on them.

For comparative purposes it is perhaps best to begin by noting that the United States spends less on social programs than almost any other Western industrialized nation.[11] In 1977, for example, the United States spent about 13.7 percent of its gross national product on income security programs (most of which, however, did not go to the poor). Among the major nations that spent more were Austria (22 percent), Belgium (25 percent), France (26 percent), West Germany (26 percent), Netherlands (28 percent), Sweden (31 percent), Switzerland (15 percent), and the United Kingdom (17 percent).

Social spending in the United States began in 1935 while the country was wrestling with the effects of the Great Depression. In 1935 the Social Security Act was established which instituted five major programs: Assistance to the Aged, Social Security, Unemployment Compensation, Aid to Dependent Children, and Aid to the Blind. These programs remained fairly small until 1964 when President Lyndon Johnson declared his "War on Poverty" with the passage of the ill-fated Economic Opportunity Act of 1964. That same year Congress established the Food Stamp Program and the following year it instituted the Medicaid and Medicare programs. Nine years later, in 1974, it enacted the Supplemental Security Income program for the aged, disabled, and the blind.

The major social programs we now have can be divided into three categories as indicated in Table 3. The most expensive of these programs are those which are NOT aimed at the poor: non-need based programs. The largest of these is social security which goes to a person whether or not the person is poor. In 1982 Social Security cost $162 billion.[12] The next most expensive program is Medicare, which also does not go to the poor. In 1982, Medicare cost $43.6 billion. The third most expensive program is unemployment compensation, which also did not go to the poor (one must first have had a job to count as "unemployed" and most of those who have held jobs are not poor). In 1982 unemployment compensation cost $25.2 billion. The total cost of non-need based programs, then, was $230.8 billion in 1982.

By contrast, need-based programs targeted at the poor are cheap.

In 1982 Aid to Families with Dependent Children cost us $8.1 billion, while Supplemental Security Income cost us $7.9 billion, for a total of $16 billion. Next cheapest are the in-kind programs for the poor, mainly Food Stamps and Medicaid. In 1982 these two programs cost a total of $29.1 billion.

TABLE 3

Social Programs by Category

(1) **Non-need-based programs:** These are paid for from employee and employer contributions; their benefits are generally wage-related. These are NOT aimed at the poor since they are not based on need. They include:
   Social Security
   Medicare
   Unemployment Compensation

(2) **Need-based cash programs:** these go to the poor who meet certain income qualifications. These are for the poor. They include:
   Aid to Families with Dependent Children (AFDC)
   Supplemental Security Income (SSI)

(3) **Need-based in-kind programs:** these also go to the poor who meet certain income qualifications. They are for the poor but provide goods instead of cash. They include:
   Food Stamps
   Medicaid

How much of the national government budget is then spent on the poor? In 1982, AFDC and SSI together accounted for about two percent of the budget. Food-stamps and Medicaid accounted for an additional four percent of the budget. If we aggregate the money from all other government social programs that go to the poor, then, an additional four percent of the national budget would be found to go to the poor. Altogether, then, about 10 percent of the budget is spent on welfare programs for the poor.

Do these programs really help the poor? They clearly have. In 1976, without these programs, 21 percent of the population would have been below the poverty level (45.8 million people). About half of these people were moved out of poverty by the cash-assistance programs. And about half of the remainder were moved out of poverty by the in-kind benefits programs. Thus, our welfare programs are responsible for yearly lifting millions of people out of destitution.

Perhaps more important, however, are the permanent effects of these programs. In 1967, before the Food Stamp and child nutrition programs were fully funded, a Field Foundation report on poverty-stricken areas in the United States found "children in significant numbers who were hungry and sick, children for whom hunger is a daily fact of life, and sickness an inevitability, . . . [children who are] weak, and apathetic, . . . suffering from hunger and disease and dying from them." Ten years later, in 1977, the Field Foundation team investigated the same areas to assess the effects of expanded government funding of food programs, and found that "it is not possible any more to find very easily the bloated bellies, the shriveled infants, the gross evidence of vitamin and protein deficiencies in children that we identified in the late 1960s."[13]

In 1963, before the 1965 implementation of Medicaid and Medicare, over 20 percent of those living under the poverty level had *never* seen a doctor despite the disproportionately high incidence of illness and disease among the poor. By 1970, as a direct result of these medical programs, only 8 percent of those in poverty still had failed to see a doctor and most of the poor—especially impoverished pregnant women—were receiving medical care proportional to that of the rest of the population. As a direct result infant mortality rates among blacks fell from 40.3 per 1000 births in 1965, to 24.2 in 1975; in the same period infant mortality rates in impoverished geographical areas were reduced by 50 percent.

Government housing programs which received increased funding during the 1960s also have had spectacular results. In 1960 some 12 percent of Americans lived in overcrowded housing (more than one person to each room); by 1976 this figure had been slashed in half and only five percent were forced to live in overcrowded conditions. In 1960 over 20 percent of the population lived in substandard housing (no plumbing or in great disrepair); by 1976 about eight percent lived in such housing.

In spite of their rather spectacular success and in spite of their relatively low cost, welfare programs for the poor are often scorned. This is perhaps largely due to a number of myths concerning these programs. Here are some examples of these false and unsupported myths:

The Myth of Dependency: Welfare makes poor people dependent on welfare, so that once they get on welfare they never get off. This myth is quite false. A 1974 study (Rydell, 1974) found that during a five-year period, only 5.7 percent of recipients remained on welfare during all five years. A 1981 study of a different sample found that only eight percent remained on welfare during a ten-year period.[14]

The Myth of Loafers: The welfare roles are full of able-bodied loafers. This is also false. The bulk of welfare recipients consist of children, then their mothers who must stay at home to raise them, then the elderly who are too old to work, and then the sick who cannot work. Less than 1% of welfare recipients are able-bodied unemployed men.[15] These men are required by law to sign up for work or work training, which they do. But because of high unemployment rates, welfare workers are not able to find work for them.

The Myth of Poor Attitudes: The poor on welfare have poor work attitudes and prefer welfare over work. This is probably the most popular falsehood spread about the poor, its popularity deriving in part from the fact that it makes us feel superior to the poor and justifies our wretched treatment of them. But every study so far has shown that there are no differences between the poor and the unpoor when it comes to life goals and wanting to work. The most recent study of this issue found that poor people on welfare feel deep shame and prefer to be off welfare and working than on welfare without work.[16] However, the study found that there are an insufficient number of jobs available at which welfare heads of households can support their families at a subsistent level. Earlier studies had also failed to find any correlations between poverty and attitudes toward work.[17]

The Myth of Welfare Cheats: A large portion of welfare people are cheats. This myth is utterly false. Welfare fraud is probably the least prevalent of all forms of fraud. Government investigations of welfare fraud have shown that only about 1/30th of one percent of all welfare cases involve some form of fraud.[18] Studies have also shown that about 40% of the population that is eligible for welfare does not accept welfare.

Conclusion

In recent years many of us have come to believe that poverty can be completely eradicated through economic growth. There is some truth to this "trickle down" theory since unemployment of the *employable poor* currently causes a great deal of poverty. However, economic growth cannot eradicate all poverty for the simple reason that the bulk of the poor, as we have seen, are *not employable.*

There is ample evidence available to demonstrate that economic growth alone cannot eradicate poverty. For example, between 1965 and 1972, real disposable per-capita income in the United States grew by 24 percent (even more than the 13 percent growth during the entire "prosperous" decade of the 1950s). If there had been *no* government spending on the poor during these years, 21.3 percent of the population would have been in poverty in 1965 and 19.2 percent would still have been in poverty in 1972. Thus, in the absence of government spending, spectacular economic growth of 24 percent reduced poverty by only 2 percentage points. However, because of government spending on welfare (including in-kind benefits), the number in poverty in 1972 was actually only nine percent. Thus, government spending was responsible for reducing poverty by 10 percentage points. Economic growth, then, alleviated poverty only marginally during this period, while welfare programs made deep cuts into poverty.[19]

The figures we reviewed at the beginning of this article explain why economic growth leaves most of the poor untouched and why welfare programs are so necessary. The bulk of the poor cannot participate in the economy because they are unemployable (they consist of single women with children, their children, the disabled, the elderly, and so on). Since they cannot participate in the economy, economic growth necessarily leaves them no better off. Only welfare programs specifically targeted at the poor—such as AFDC, SSI, the Food Stamp program, and Medicaid—can alleviate the poverty of the millions upon millions of impoverished men, women, and children who now live in the United States.

God help us if these millions continue poor because of our lack of knowledge of their plight, and because of our unwillingness to provide for them. Isaiah in the Old Testament, speaking for the God of the Jews, cries out, "I will hide my eyes from you even though you make many prayers; I will not listen, your hands are full of blood; learn to do good, to seek justice, to correct oppression, to defend the fatherless, and to plead for the widow" (Is. 1:15-17). Several centuries later, Jesus, speaking for the same God, said, "Depart from me, you cursed, into eternal fire; for I was hungry and you gave me no food, thirsty and you gave me no drink, naked and you did not clothe me, sick and you did not visit me; for whatever you did not do to one of the least of these, you did not do to me" (Mt. 25:41-45).

Notes

[1]Unless otherwise noted, all statistics in this article are drawn from two sources: all current figures are taken from U.S. Bureau of the Census, *Current Population Reports, Money Income and Poverty Status of Families and Persons in the United States: 1983 (Advance Data From the March 1984 Current Population Survey)*; earlier figures are drawn from U.S. Bureau of the Census, *Statistical Abstract of the United States, 1984*.

[2]Michael Harrington, *The New American Poverty* (New York: Holt, Rinehart, and Winston, 1984), pp. 69-71.

[3]U.S. Bureau of the Census, *Alternative Methods for Valuing Selected In-Kind Transfer Benefits and Measuring their Effect on Poverty*, 1982.

[4]*Wall Street Journal*, "U.S. Poverty Rate Increased, Study Shows, When Value of Non-Cash Aid Was Counted", February 24, 1984, p. 16.

[5]These figures are drawn from the sources in note 1.

[6]*San Francisco Examiner*, "Millions of Children Make Up the Nation's New Poor", December 23, 1984, pp. 1 and 20.

[7]See note 6.

[8]Leonard Goodwin, *Causes and Cures of Welfare* (Lexington, MA: Lexington Books, 1983).

[9]Martha S. Hill, Daniel H. Hill, and James N. Morgan, eds., *Five Thousand American Families*, vol. IX (Ann Arbor, MI: The University of Michigan, 1981), p. 140.

[10]Harrington, *The New American Poverty*, pp. 14-38.

[11]H.R. Rodgers Jr., *The Cost of Human Neglect* (Armonk, NY: W.E. Sharpe Inc., 1982), p. 51.

[12]See Rodgers, *The Cost of Human Neglect*, chapter 3.

[13]For the data in this and the following paragraphs see John E. Schwarz, *America's Hidden Success* (New York: W.W. Norton & Company, 1983), pp. 29-59.

[14]Peter Rydell, *et al.*, *Welfare Caseload Dynamics in New York City* (New York: The Rand Corporation, 1974); Hill, Hill, and Morgan, *Five Thousand American Families*, vol. IX, chapter 4.

[15]Joseph Julian, *Social Problems* (Englewood Cliffs, NJ: Prentice-Hall, Inc., 1977), p. 261.

[16]Goodwin, *The Causes and Cures of Welfare*.

[17]Leonard Goodwin, *Do the Poor Want Work?* (Washington, D.C.: The Brookings Institution, 1972); Charles Davidson and Charles M. Goetz, "Are the Poor Different?" *Social Problems*, 22 (1974): 229.

[18]Briar, "Welfare From Below", *California Law Review*, (1966), 54, note 16.

[19]Schwarz, *America's Hidden Success*, pp. 33-35.

CAUSES AND EFFECTS OF POVERTY AND POSSIBLE SOLUTIONS

Michael Harrington

A French writer, Serge Milano, in a recent book on poverty writes that there is no such thing as poverty; there are, rather, poverties. Poverty, he writes, is constantly being redefined. It is neither a stable fact nor a phenomenon of social life. Milano suggests that in the middle of the 19th century, poverty was proletarianization. It was the emergence of the industrial capitalist society: it was the gigantic cities, the child labor, the 14 hour work days. It was a phase of the system.

What Milano speaks of is the poverty of Friedrich Engels, Charles Dickens, Victor Hugo, not the kind of poverty that exists in the United States today. The kinds of poverty that exist here today are many.

There is the poverty of the Great Depression. It was a majority poverty. And there was the poverty of the 1960s, which we very self-consciously defined in the preface to the Economic Opportunity Act of 1964, as a paradox in the midst of abundance. (In the middle of the most successful economic decade in the history of this society, we said poverty was an accident.)

The normal condition of American society is no longer poverty as it was during the Depression. In the 1980s, there are some people who have been left behind: they live in Appalachia, Harlem, the south side of Chicago, in the barrios of Los Angeles and New York City. Indeed, poverty in the 1980s is different than all those other poverties. In the United States today, poverty is a dynamic reality, not a static concept.

How do we define poverty? There is in the United States today something called, erroneously, the poverty line. It is determined by the federal government and where it fatefully falls marks where the money does or does not go. Therefore, it is a very serious matter. But there is not actually a poverty line. For an urban family of four the poverty line is drawn at a $10,000 a year income.

But there are many poverty lines. There is a different line for an urban family of three than for an urban family of eight or for a rural family of two. The standard poverty line is drawn for an urban family of four. The definition of this poverty line was first worked out by Mollie Orshansky who worked for the Social Security Administration. She did this under the aegis of John Kennedy and later Lyndon Johnson during 1963-64 at the time of the rediscovery of poverty. Her definition was based on food. Orshansky defined poverty by taking as the base of our definition a meal. (Actually, she took three different meals, and originally came up with three different poverty lines. The meal was a meal that would hold body and soul together, that would not cause you to get ill or die; an emergency meal.) She took three different meals because what kind of meal will hold body and soul together without harming you is debatable. And the government picked the cheapest of the three (because the government has an interest in not defining too many people as poor, particularly if it is going to cost money). Orshansky took that meal and multiplied its cost by three. She did that because a study in 1955 in the Eisenhower years showed that for poor people the ratio of income spent on food to total income was one-third. So you multiplied the food cost by three and you came up with a poverty line for an urban family of four which ever since has been corrected for inflation, although the meal has not been upgraded.

In sum, our poverty line is based on a 1964 definition of what a good meal is, and uses 1984 prices. That is what is meant when we say 15.3 percent of the American people (about 35 million) are poor. In recent years, starting in the 1970s, this definition has been criticized. (The critique was eventually picked up by the Congressional Budget Office.) Critics claimed the definition of poverty was made solely in terms of cash income.

Some of the best things we have done for the poor since we discovered or rediscovered poverty in the early 60s have been not in terms of cash, but in-kind goods and services. We have created the food stamp program, which came out of the work of Robert Kennedy, George McGovern, and other liberals in the mid- and late-60s, and which is one of the major programs affecting the poor in America today.

So these critics said: why don't we take the cash value of food stamps, the cash value of Medicaid, the cash value of rental subsidies, compute them, add them to the cash income of the poor, and say that the real income of the poor is not their cash income, but cash income plus the cash value of the goods and services they get from things like food stamps and Medicaid?

That is a legitimate criticism. It is not, however, as simple as that. It is simple enough to estimate the cash value of one dollar in food stamps. (One dollar of food stamps will buy you one dollar of groceries.) But what is the value of a dollar of Medicaid? That gets a little trickier. Those who make this argument assume that every single dollar of Medicaid is spent with 100 percent efficiency. But, in fact, forty percent of Medicaid is spent on the care of dying people. Medicare does not pay for nursing homes. If you get to the point where you have serious medical problems and you need around the clock care, you do not qualify under Medicare. So you pauperize yourself; you give away everything. And then you will qualify for Medicaid payments for your nursing home. Do you know that we now spend one percent of the gross national product of the United States on the last year of life? How are we to deal with the statistical anomaly that an aging person in the United States who suffers a long, agonizing last year of life can statistically enter the middle class because of that fact? Should we really take those billions of dollars and add them to the income of the poor?

These critics who one day say the federal government is rife with bureaucracy and inefficiency say the next, when defining poverty, that the federal government acts perfectly. In the mid-1970s, and still in the 1980s, one received credit in this society for proving there are fewer poor people than usually perceived; in the 60s one got credit for proving there were more. This might suggest that if statistics can so change with the moods of the decades, statistics is not an exact science. Some analysts look only for the overestimations of poverty, not the underestimations. We do not know how many poor people there are, but there are more than estimations show; they are called undocumented workers.

In California these undocumented workers are primarily from Mexico and Central and South America; in the East they are primarily from the Caribbean. They are very poor; they work in sweatshops in this era of the microchip; and, they are not statistics because they do not want to be statistics. Nobody has ever bothered about counting them in. Nobody wants to remember that Mollie Orshansky, as she herself admitted, estimated too low. The fact is that the official definition of 15.3 percent of American society as poor is a moderate estimate. I do not think it is an overestimation; if anything, it is an underestimation.

What are the dynamics of poverty and what causes it? The composition of the poor has changed; they are different now than they were twenty years ago. Some of them are working people. Some are people from relatively well-paid smokestack industries who belong to unions like the United Automobile Workers and the United Steel Workers. When I was working on my most recent book [*The New American Poverty*], I was out in Mckeesport, Pennsylvania, talking to steelworkers. I talked to people who made $30,000 a year at their last jobs, and who because they lost their medical coverage along with their job, could not take their children to a doctor unless it were an emergency.

Does that mean that all of the people who were unemployed in the 1982-83 recession became poor? Of course not; they are a minority. But a minority either did become poor or was in danger of becoming poor.

Last November [1984], even as we celebrated the enormous creation of jobs in the United States, the Bureau of labor statistics came out with analyses of people whose jobs had been destroyed. Between January 1979 and January 1984, 5.1 million American workers saw their jobs disappear. They were not laid off temporarily, rather, the plant shut down and the job simply disappeared. The Bureau of Labor Statistics tried to follow these people and found that about 60 percent found new jobs with a significant pay cut. They were not unemployed, just pushed down. The Bureau also found that 25 percent of those 5.1 million workers in January 1984 were still unemployed. Fifteen percent had left the labor market altogether.

There is a problem of poverty for a class of people who thought they had it made—those trade union, smokestack, blue-collar workers shakily employed by disappearing industries. There are also the undocumented in the United States. Ironically, the Reagan administration has told us what a poverty problem they have. When Simpson-Mazzoli, the law on trying to deal with amnesty, identification cards, etc., was being debated before the Congress, the administration hesitated, stating, in effect: if we have an amnesty for all those undocumented people, that will be an enormous welfare cost because once we give them amnesty they qualify for our social programs.

There is a population in the United States, some of them working in sweatshops (and there are known sweatshops in all of the major cities in the United States, including San Francisco and New York), terrified people who cannot complain about their working conditions because if they do the employer can turn them over to immigration and get them kicked out of the society. Rather than be deported, they will work for less than minimum wage, twelve hours a day, and take home piecework for their kids to do at night. They prefer that to being sent back to wherever they came from. That is a second group arising from the micro-electric age.

Another group is the homeless. Some of the homeless are there because of good intentions—such as de-institutionalization—that were never acted upon. Under John Kennedy we said: "We will de-institutionalize these people from the snake pits we put them into, and we will bring them back into the society where the society will greet them." We did de-institutionalize them, but not much else.

So we have people, the walking wounded of our society with deep emotional and mental problems on the streets. The way to deal with these people is not to send them back to the institutions. Only about a third of the homeless are those de-institutionalized mental patients. A lot of them are working families, or younger people who have been taken out of single room occupancy hotels so that room could be made for condominiums. Single room occupancy hotels were one of the places where the welfare poor, not the ex-mental patients, but standard, ordinary poor could live. But the single room occupancy hotel, once an institution, has been turned into a place for rich people. There is no room at the inn, so to speak.

Then there is the tremendous increase in the number of women among the poor. It has been referred to as the "feminization of poverty." It has to do partly with economics. That is to say, among the poor the economic possibility of fatherhood is nowhere near as good as the biological possibility of fatherhood. But it also has to do with the general deterioration of values in American society, a deterioration of values which is expressed in the upper class in different ways: in cocaine and divorce. Among the poor the problem is similar, but expressed differently: in something like teenage pregnancy.

That relates to another terribly frightening aspect of the poverty of the 1980s: it is striking the young. The poverty of the 1960s hit the elderly mostly. One of the great accomplishments of American society in the past twenty years is that we have cut the poverty of the aging in half. We did so by universalizing social security and indexing its benefits. So now only 15 percent of the aging are poor, rather than a third. But now 15.3 percent of the American *people* are poor, 20 percent of the American people under the age of sixteen are poor, 25 percent of the American people under the age of six are poor.

There is also in the United States now a rural poverty which sometimes comes from rural gentrification. I was up in Maine talking to some people working with the rural poor, for example. And they told me it becomes a problem when middle-class city dwellers decide they would like to have a charming farm in Maine as a second or third home. On that whim, a farm is taken out of the agricultural economy—and perhaps destroys the economic livelihood of a group of people scratching out a life—and pushes the previous owners into a decaying mill town in Maine.

Why do we have a "new" poverty? First of all, we are going through a shift in the international division of labor the likes of which we have not known in this world for a hundred years. The United States is about to import automobiles from South Korea. The South Koreans now make steel more efficiently than both the United States and the Japanese. Thus, the smokestack industries of the United States which were the backbone of the American working class—the jobs which allowed the poor to get out of the menial jobs into better paid jobs—those industries, those jobs are declining. The UAW contract with General Motors and Ford last year was about as much as the UAW can get, and the deal was that in return for Ford and GM taking care of the existing membership of the UAW, immunizing them from technological unemployment, the UAW would let GM and Ford do anything they wanted to do with robots and automation.

The impact of robots and of automation will not be felt by the current members of the UAW, but by those who if this were not happening might have become members of the UAW, those who would have escaped poverty that way.

A recent article in *Business Week* describes GM's new automobile, the Saturn, as the first new General Motors car since the Chevrolet in 1918. GM's aim is to have that automobile produced by robots.

Right now there are 55 labor hours per car in the United States; the makers of the Saturn aim to reduce that number to 21.

We have, in other words, a shift in the international division of labor, related to a technological revolution which strikes smokestack America which is going to strike at the office which is going to strike at the service sector, which is going to strike even in the executive suite. Finally, there is the multinationalization of corporate capital. And capital pits American workers against foreign workers to the detriment of both.

Capital can increase American poverty and impede an integrated economic development in the Third World at the same time. These are the factors that are making the new poverty so much more difficult to deal with. The Department of Labor recently came out with a study on which jobs would grow the most between 1982 and 1995. The top growth job, with about 750,000 new jobs created in that period, was building custodians. In the top ten, there were about three relatively well-paid jobs: school teachers, truck drivers, and registered nurses. The rest of the rapidly increasing jobs were nurses aides and orderlies, waiters, and waitresses, office clerks, and so on. In the forty jobs that would grow the most between now and 1995, only two jobs had anything to do with computers. Those two jobs were programmers and analysts.

We are moving toward a three-level society, separate and unequal: a top, 20-25 percent of the population, those with the high tech jobs, the information jobs; a middle, where the blue-collar workers are, those who do not get pushed down into poverty but slide down; and a bottom.

In the 1960s, there was a program aimed at getting the automobile companies to hire the unemployed in Detroit. I was critical of it because the program gave federal subsidies to the automobile companies for hiring the hard core unemployed. It seemed to me the automobile companies were so up against the wall looking for workers that they would have hired them anyway. But in Detroit in 1967, we actually created new blue collar, United Automobile Worker jobs for mainly black unemployed people from the ghetto of Detroit. That could not be done today; there are no more such jobs. The dynamics of poverty in the United States are such that the elimination of poverty is much more difficult today than it was twenty years ago.

Charles Murray, in *Losing Ground* presents a scene many people really believe in. In his book, Murray wonders: why do we have so many poor people today? What is the cause of the persistence of poverty? Because, he claims, the War on Poverty unwittingly created work disincentives. We allowed, and even encouraged, people to withdraw from the labor market. That is the real tragedy; it is the "liberal Vietnam"—liberals, trying to abolish poverty, created it.

Murray's answer, then, is to abolish all social programs for working-age people. He wants to abolish food stamps, AFDC, unemployment compensation, workman's compensation. When somebody claims a single cause for a complex phenomenon, he or she is probably wrong. Murray does not look at technological revolution; he does not consider that the unemployment rate is much higher now in a period of recovery than it was in the 1960s. He does not look at a changing occupational structure. He simply says it is the social programs which motivated people to drop out of the labor force that is the root of the persistence of poverty.

Murray takes black male labor force participation as the chief item in his case. Basically what he said was: "Let blacks stand for the poor. Let black males stand for blacks. Let us now look at black labor force participation, and what do we discover? We discover that in 1964 black and white males had almost exactly the same rate of labor force participation." In the 1970s, the black labor force participation rate dropped about 14 percent, the white by seven. Murray concludes from this that the programs that started in 1968-69 created disincentives for these workers. But more black males left the labor force before the liberal programs were enacted. Indeed, social programs did not create disincentives. Statistics also show that the labor participation of black women increased during those years.

Perhaps Lyndon Johnson is partly to blame for this. A lot of Americans think we spent an enormous amount of money on the poor. We had a War on Poverty, we had a Great Society, we gave all this money away to the poor. But the fact is the overwhelming bulk of federal expenditures on social programs are age-tested not means-tested; two thirds of domestic social spending goes to Social Security. Even though Johnson sometimes talked as if he were remaking the universe every morning, we never spent much money on the poor.

Indeed, I wish I could have been there the moment when it finally got through to Reagan that you cannot balance the budget on the backs of the poor because we never spent enough money on them in the first place. Also, all the social programs of the 1960s for the poor were failures. (Such as job training programs that trained people for jobs that did not exist.) But the more evidence we get, the more we see that these programs paid off. Excessive liberalism does not cause poverty. The cause of the persistence of poverty is the defects of anti-poverty programs. The basic causes of poverty are massive structural changes which threaten to turn this society into three unequal societies.

How do we deal with these problems? I must tell you that though I am a radical, I am frightened by how radical we have to be to deal with these problems. I do not think, with Reagan's America, we are going to deal with them in the immediate future. For example, the bishops, in their pastoral letter, talk about the need to get unemployment down to three or four percent. To get unemployment that low we have to do some innovative things. One of the saddest intellectual histories in American society is the history of the concept of full employment. In the early 60s, under Kennedy and Johnson, we had something called the full employment-unemployment rate. We defined full employment by a rate of unemployment. We said it was three to four percent. Under Nixon we raised the rate of tolerable, acceptable unemployment, and changed the name from the full employment-unemployment rate to the "high" employment rate. Now we have raised the rate again; it cannot get much below seven percent.

This is now termed the "inflation threshold" unemployment rate. The employment rate is defined in terms of inflation, not in terms of unemployment—a total turning around of values. We cannot deal with racism, sexism, and poverty in the United States unless we get unemployment rates down. How is it that, although blacks and other minorities are a minority of the poor, they are disproportionately poor? One-third of the total black population is poor, 12 percent of whites are poor, but there are more whites than blacks.

Even though there is a distinct racist aspect to the problem of poverty, unemployment, and almost any other problem you can mention in the United States, is an integrated problem. How do we deal with the racist aspect of it?

In his book, *Window of Opportunity*, self-styled right wing populist, Newt Gingrich, a member of the United States Congress, presents the weirdest combination of left and right I have ever encountered. (It seems to have been written by Tom Hayden of 1965 and

Jerry Falwell.) For example, Gingrich proposed that we take basic foods, like beans, rice, cheese, etc. and make them available free in every grocery store in the United States. He wants to get rid of food stamps because he does not want the poor to be able to choose anything more than beans and rice and cheese. In order to get rid of food stamps, he is willing to make these things free (a socialist principle coming from a conservative).

Gingrich has now made the feeling more passionate in me that the government has to, among other things, create jobs. If we accept the normal, natural trends of the American economy (which really do not exist); if we take those projections of the Department of Labor as fate, there will be more poverty in 1995 than in 1985. The occupational structure of the United States is something in which we must intervene; we have to create jobs, good jobs. If the economy is not creating good jobs, then the society has to create good jobs if it wants to abolish poverty.

Thus, there must be, first, enormous tax subsidies for any corporation that will create new jobs in an area of high unemployment and poverty. Second, there must be planned investments that create new jobs such as a rail system that is as good as those in France and Italy. We could put thousands to work building something that people would want to pay for which would finance itself.

To deal with poverty, we are going to have to be more radical than we have been. Suppose that, as I think is going to be the case, there is a recession within the next two years. Ronald Reagan's 1984 campaign was, in the words of my Jesuit education, a monument to the fallacy *post-hoc-ergo-propter-hoc*. That is to say, because the rain dance occurred before the rain, the rain dance is the cause of the rain. Because supply-side economics and Ronald Reagan existed before the recovery, supply-side economics and Ronald Reagan are the cause of the recovery. The fact is, the recovery occurred in spite of Reagan and supply-side economics, and was clearly a demand-side recovery.

But supposing that in the middle of 1986 we have a moderate recession, unemployment goes up by only 2.5 percent to 9.5. Supposing that Reagan actually gets some deficit reduction prior to then and our deficit at that point is only $200 billion. A one percent increase in unemployment in terms of lost government revenue and increased government outlays increases the deficit more or less by about 30 billion. (The Reagan people would say 25; they are low.)

So, let us hypothesize. We have a 2.5 percent in unemployment on top of a $200 billion deficit; we are now at a $275 billion deficit. What do you propose to do? More deficit financing? At that point the Republican fear of the last fifteen years becomes true because of what the Republicans have done: the deficit is so high that the financing of the deficit crowds the private sector out of the money market. And rather than being a cure for recession, deficit financing could be the cause of increased recession and unemployment. What do you do? At that point—and I am talking about something that could occur in the next 14, 15, or 16 months—we are looking at the need not to redistribute income and wealth, which I am very much for, but simply to undo the reactionary regressive distribution that Reagan imposed in 1981.

There is no way to solve these problems unless you are willing to get the rich off of welfare. There is no way to do it. And this society, I am afraid, gets nervous when you talk that way. It is thought of as the language of conflict. Indeed, it is.

Out of this crisis, and not simply in terms of poverty but even in terms of college students in the Silicon Valley, we must redefine the working life. I think on the 100th anniversary of the American Federation of Labor's proclamation in 1886 of the struggle for the eight hour day, that we have to place on the agenda the struggle for the 32 hour week. On the basis of a 40 hour week we cannot deal with the unemployment and poverty problems of this society.

When we talk about the problem of working life, we do not talk about it simply in terms of the poor, although it concerns them. We have to talk about it as it is relevant to all of us.

Finally, we cannot solve the problem of American poverty at the expense of world poverty. The notion that justice in the Third World could be an engine of economic growth and employment in the First World is not contradictory. Those who counterpose the two are the multinational corporations which play the two worlds off against each other. What we must find is some way of cooperatively making it in the interests of people in Mexico and Latin America and Asia and Africa and in the United States to have a common interest in the development of the Third World.

If you ask American workers today why they are menaced or threatened, they will say, it is because of the Japanese, the South Koreans, the Mexicans, the Brazilians, the Argentinians. They often see Third World workers as enemies. But there is a politics that can make the elimination of poverty in the United States and the elimination of poverty in the world not antithetical but able to reinforce each other.

The facts of poverty are debatable, but the fact of poverty in the United States is huge and has not been overestimated. The theory that poverty is the result of liberal programs is well-intentioned, but absurd. The real cause of the persistence of poverty in the 1980s is the enormous structural changes in the American and world economy.

Finally, a word about the bishops' pastoral. When William Simon says to the bishops: "You people should stick to your sermons. Talk about the other world," he says in effect that although economists and business people may be religious, the economy is agnostic; there are no values in the economy. Simon has it that there can be no values in economic thought, that it is wrong to invoke the Judeo-Christian tradition, that it is wrong to insist that one measure of society's economic progress in terms of the poor and not simply in terms of GNP. But one has to understand that the very notion of GNP is a value-laden notion. Where is it written that any increase in material wealth including an increase in material wealth that increased premature death by cancer, is an advance? Where is it set down that an increase in wealth which is accompanied by an increase in the severity of poverty is an advance? One of the most important things the bishops have done and one of the most important things that all of us must do after having carefully and in the most scrupulous way looked at the facts and made our analysis, is look at this economy as a field in which values have to come into play. And one of the most crucial values of all is the abolition of poverty in this country and in the world.

REDISTRIBUTION TO THE POOR:
A COLLECTIVE EXPRESSION
OF INDIVIDUAL ALTRUISM

Kenneth Arrow

What justifications do we have for a government policy of redistribution—a program which would tax the well-off and transfer payments to the worse off?

There is a common view, latent in the popular feeling and expressed by certain philosophers and economists, that you really should not redistribute income. Income is private property; whatever somebody gets is whatever he or she should get. Some people say *deserve*, some people say it does not matter whether the recipient deserves it or not, private property must be respected.

Contrary to a number of opposing views, and in line with some others, the morality of redistribution is an individual matter. Generally, people are concerned about the welfare of others; but, like a lot of other collective concerns, it can only be implemented through collective action, which in the modern world takes the form typically of state action. There are other forms of collective action, voluntary collaboration of one kind or another, and they are very important. But the dominant form has become state action whether we like it or not, and therefore the responsibility about caring for others is much more efficiently done through a common mechanism, a collective mechanism, than it is through individual mechanisms.

It is on this basis, that redistribution of income expresses a significant part of our individual values, that the concern for others in need expressed by state redistribution can best be defended.

Most defenses of the ethics of redistribution start with the welfare of the individual as the unit of analysis. A typical criterion that economists are prone to use (and if it has its limits, it also has its value), is the concept of efficiency. The technical definition of efficiency is sometimes referred to by the name of the first person to formulate it explicitly, the Italian Vilfredo Pareto.

We say that a state of affairs is inefficient. It is a rather negative definition: a state is efficient if there is no way of changing it to make everybody better off. Of course, this state may be quite unjust; somebody may be very well off, and other people very poorly off, but at least it is efficient. Most advice economists give—deregulation, to take something fairly prominent—currently has tended to be in terms of efficiency.

Efficiency arguments are sometimes used to justify state intervention because some things cannot be done by individuals. But the evaluating mechanism, the way in which we judge efficiency, is based on an individual's judgment. And we do not each, even as individuals, judge things solely by consequences to ourselves; rather, we are all members, one of another.

The boundaries between individuals are not rigid; they are fluid. I am not arguing that society can have values independent of the people in it. Though I want to play down the individual as the object of welfare propositions, I do not want to abolish it, I want to point out the independence of individuals. Another point I want to stress is the role of the individual as the subject, as the one who makes the welfare proposition. In other words, I want to ground the argument on the basis of individual preferences; preferences which have an altruistic component. I want to take individual moralities as given, and draw the consequences of that fact. The emphasis is then on how we can frame institutions so as to best realize individual moral judgments.

Let me revert to the question of efficiency. We do have an argument that a free market—what we call technically a competitive equilibrium—will generally lead to efficient use of the resources we have. But this is true only in certain circumstances, namely, where our actions do not directly impinge on the welfare of others. When an action directly impinges on the welfare of others, we call it an externality, a phrase you may have heard making its way into the popular press.

This issue usually comes up in connection with pollution. If I drive an automobile, I may create certain wastes in the exhaust which cause some people's eyes to tear, or perhaps affect the longevity of people subject to emphysema or other diseases of the lungs. There are a large number of similar problems. If these problems did not exist, we could say the free market operates. Why does it not operate here? It is because this cost that is being imposed on others is not priced. The imposer of the cost does not directly have to pay for it. You emit the smoke, you impinge on other people's welfare, but you're not required to pay for it, so you engage in these activities more than might be desired. To minimize at least these externalities, you may have to create substitutes for the market in those areas. These might take the form of regulation—and we have a series of regulations on safety and health, pollution limits, and so forth. They may take the form of taxes. Instead of regulating undesirable activities, activities which impose cost on others, you may simply tax those costs. (This is one of the justifications for high tax on alcohol.) Or, we may not use the government, but rely on social conventions. It is wrong to litter. Avoidance of litter may be enforced as much by self-control and morality, a kind of a social convention, as it is by the government.

The problem of externality is what is sometimes called the free rider. I would like the pollution to be lower because other people are polluting me. They would like me to pollute less. From my point of view, my pollution affects me only insignificantly. It effects everybody. I am going to make a very small difference, virtually none at all, in the total level of pollution. So I will not feel constrained, if I were not otherwise hemmed in, to lower my pollution levels because it does not hurt me very much and I may be getting some pleasure out of the activity, driving faster, buying cheaper gasoline.

Nevertheless, if we all agree to reduce the pollution emitted, then we would all be better off, because the pleasure I get out of this additional activity is not worth as much as the reduction in pollution from everybody else's refraining. This is an example where everyone is individually motivated to engage in antisocial activities. But if we can get together and form a binding agreement, we would all be better off. In other words, efficiency requires some kind of action other than the market. This social agreement might take various forms, as I mentioned, social norms, or taxes, or regulation.

Some of the trends in current ethical theory start with selfish individuals—individuals thought of as hard, massy atoms, bouncing off each other, but not interacting, not really caring. In these theories, morality is essentially a form of extended prudence. I have already referred to the simple criterion of efficiency. We began with individuals concerned only with their own welfare. Even when there are externalities, the concern of the individual is still with his or her own welfare: I accept the idea of regulation of pollution because I'm going to be better off by it.

So the logic, even in the case of externalities, is the same as it is for the free market where there are no externalities. It does not go beyond the efficiency criterion, which is very weak. As we have seen, it does not really discuss redistribution at all.

Another traditional philosophy, utilitarianism, starts with the individual getting satisfaction out of his or her own consumption: what I get is what I value. But, if you look at it from society's point of view, you've got to look at everybody. As one of the great founders of utilitarianism, Jeremy Bentham, said: each one should count for one and only one. What you ought to do is to calculate how much satisfaction a person gets, add up these satisfactions, and then say, "well, we want to make that sum of satisfactions as big as possible."

This idea of satisfaction usually means, though not always, an equalizing of income. The argument is based on the observation that an additional dollar of income means less to a rich person than to a poor person. Start off with a very unequal distribution of income and take a dollar away from a rich person and give it to a poor person. Matters are likely to be better off because presumably the value of that last dollar to the rich person is pretty low, whereas it may be quite high to the poor person. Utilitarianism, then seems to lead to a case of equalization of income. There are some who have used utilitarianism arguments but have not come to this egalitarian conclusion; they say that the rich, with their refined tastes are more sensitive; that they can feel more strongly the difference an additional dollar makes. This argument has not been advanced much in recent years, though you will find it in late 19th century Victorian England.

However, apart from these particular questions the whole approach has found itself a little dimmed for epistomological reasons. What do these utilities mean? How would you go about measuring them? What experiment could we perform which would tell us whether one person enjoys income more than another? What are these satisfactions I'm adding up? I do not see them, I cannot feel them, how would I know what they are? That is one question.

Another question: why is there an obligation on me to to make the sum of satisfactions in society high?

Suppose I am rich. Someone says if I take $100 from you and give it to someone down the street then obviously society is going to be better off. I might say, okay, you have convinced me it is true. What of it? Why is that justification for my giving up those dollars?

There is a counter argument sometimes called, the veil of ignorance, a name given by John Rawls. It questions the meaning of a moral decision. It states that a decision is moral regardless of the circumstances; it is moral if it is good for everybody.

What does that mean? Consider: I do not know who I am. Imagine my thinking about moral questions, say about the distribution of income, before I know who I am, when I am still behind the veil of ignorance. Before I was born, so to speak, I did not know which state in society I was going to have. I say I could be anybody in society. What decision would I make about, let us say, the redistribution of income, before I know where I stand? This argument, in the hands of Rawls and some economists such as William Vickre, John Marsanyi has led to interesting instructions and effects. One way of interpreting the utility of income, is to put yourself in the place of someone who would receive that income. It is a kind of extended sympathy viewpoint. Rawls has developed this most richly and has a strong argument for redistribution based on it. But it still assumes each individual is selfish. It holds that your concern for others is not a concern as such, but rather an admission that you do not know who you are—that you are providing for another because that person could have been you.

That is a coherent theory, but meanwhile, we are here, we are not behind a veil of ignorance. You might be able to say, I have learned who I am, I am successful. Why should I give to others?

The selfishness hypothesis has been basic to what I call positive economics. The tendency of economists has been to assume selfishness. This assumption leads to a theory that explains a great deal and leaves a great deal unexplained. Economists, after having somewhat of a heyday of reputation, are somewhat put down by the press. It turns out that the selfishness hypothesis is not a consistently successful thing. There are certain areas within the realms of our observation where it fails, although it does succeed in many ways.

Rawls had a problem when trying to apply his veil of ignorance theory to saving. He wound up with the view that the only thing that matters in society is the welfare of the worst off person. If that

were true, why ever save for the future? Why benefit future genera-
tions? Over time, each generation will be better off than its prede-
cessor. So why should anybody save for people who are going to be
better off than you anyway?

Why do people save at all? Maybe anxiety about post-retirement
income. But that hardly explains the saving that really goes on. It
also would suggest that there is concern for the family, which
shoots a hole into the idea of total selfishness. The idea that people
are interdependent, that their wants, needs, and cares are interdependent, is not a new theme; it is common among ethical thinkers—
St. Paul, Aristotle (who said "man is a social animal"). The Jewish
sage Hillel was asked two pertinent questions: If I am not for
myself, then who is for me? And if I am not for others, who am I?

I think those questions sum up the point. There are two points
that are relevant here. One is that people as moral beings have a
moral component to their preferences. I think that it is a fact, not
an ought-to-be, but a fact. On the other hand, it is also true that
people are selfish, that their concern for themselves is greater than
their concern for others. It would be very unreasonable, essentially
inhuman, for a person to think of himself as one person in a four
billion member society, and regard his own welfare as no more
important than anyone else's. It is an extreme which denies individ-
uality.

On the opposite extreme, the belief that only you count in a
world of many is equally false. It is in the intermediate realm that I
find the argument for redistribution.

A fine book by the English sociologist, Richard Titmuss, *The Gift
Relation*, compares the blood supply in the United Kingdom to that
of the United States. Titmuss found that more blood was given in
England—enough in fact to sustain all medical needs in England
where the supply of blood is strictly voluntary—than in this country
where about 50% of the blood is commercially priced and 50% is
given voluntarily.

Personal caring is a genuine fact. People are not giving away
large amounts of their money, but they are giving, even on a voluntary basis. The preferences of a person, what the economists would
call the utilities of the individual, include what the individual will
privately get, but they will also include, though with so much smaller weight, the consumption levels of others.

This has been formulated in some terms by economists, but
they have not followed through the logic as much as might be. Now,

if we think of this as impersonal giving, we have to assume that the others are treated more or less alike. I do not really know who is benefitting. I may care for others, but my caring is more or less parcelled evenly among all other individuals. Each individual has a utility function, which may be thought of as the views of that individual, of ego, as I will call it, on the social plane. The ego's views include a pretty healthy component of consumption by ego but also a component of the consumption of the welfare levels of all other individuals; if left to him or herself, a person might take a large amount for ego, and leave a relatively small amount for others. A pie needs to be divided, and society has to agree how to divide the pie. For the purpose of just trying to isolate values, what people want, we will think of the pie as given, the amount available as given to be divided. Now, we must form a social judgment. Each person has preferences for the division, but these preferences do involve, as I say, concern for others; even a dictator will not take it all. This is where the theory of externalities comes in. If I am concerned about the welfare of others, I know that everyone is concerned. If I take any particular other, everybody is concerned about that other. So we will all get satisfaction if that other were made better off.

Therefore, for any one of us to benefit from the other, we give some contribution to welfare, but only a small part. If I give a dollar to an other, I get some satisfaction out of that, though less in general than I would if I kept it myself, unless I am very wealthy. When I am wealthy enough, I will give to others. But if I agree to give a dollar on the condition that everybody else in the large group gives a dollar, then that agreement will make all of us better off. Each of us benefits from the dollars given out by others. The satisfaction from redistributing to the poor goes to every member of the society. Therefore, giving to the poor is essentially an externality, something we can achieve collectively, not individually. Hence, there becomes a great value to income equality. No matter how selfish each ego is, if we accept that the selfishness has limits, a redistribution of income to the poor will benefit all of us.

Indeed, if we assume the pie is fixed so that the redistribution of income does not itself reduce the size of the pie, it can be shown, mathematically that the efficient allocation is going to be essentially egalitarian. If any significant number of people are significantly above the average, that group will gain by voluntarily agreeing to transfer, because each one member of the group gains by the fact that other members of the group are giving.

We should not go for complete equality because some redistribution will take place through taxes and transfers. And taxes and transfers may have significant effects at reducing the size of the pie. If everyone is guaranteed an income, no one will work.

The egalitarian allocation is efficient in the terms I have been using, with regard to the satisfaction individuals have, including, of course, their moral satisfaction, i.e., the satisfaction derived from the well-being of others. But, like any other form of externality, collective action is required.

If each person individually is giving, then it would pay for any individual not to give at all. Essentially there is a free-rider aspect to voluntary giving, but it is removed by collective action. Moral judgments exist; people do act morally to some extent, and from that there is a large degree of collective satisfaction properly expressed in a binding agreement to redistribute income to the poor. Therefore, it seems, present trends are moving in an inefficient direction.

II. Political Perspectives

POLITICS AND POVERTY

Julian Bond

In the last four years, the number of people living in poverty in America has increased by more than 5 million, from 29.3 million in 1980 to 34.4 million today. The 15% poverty rate these people represent is the highest since 1965, when the war on poverty formally began. In sum, current federal policies have wiped out 15 years of progress in reducing poverty.

Yet we Americans remain ambivalent about fighting poverty and unsure of its cause or cure. Our national leadership tells us that government has barely any role to play in feeding the hungry or housing the homeless, and that any effort to do so simply destroys the ability and desire of the poor to help themselves. They tell us that food stamps for hungry children help create the staggering deficit. And they tell us that the market system—not government assistance—is the surest way to provide jobs and income for the poor. These statements are all untrue, but because the people who espouse them sit in seats of power, they threaten to become a permanent part of American life and to do even more harm to the helpless.

There have been two major occasions in the 20th century when the destitute became disorderly through politics or protest—in the '30s and in the '60s when public relief measures were adopted as a partial means of regulating the poor. When the turbulence subsided, the welfare system subsided as well and became a partial means of regulating labor. The able-bodied poor were forced off the relief rolls and into the large pool of unorganized cheap labor. The remainder became a pariah class of supposed sluggards and drones.

But these anti-poverty efforts—during the Depression and again, beginning in the 1960s—helped immeasurably to lighten the burden of poverty, and correct the systemic weaknesses of American capitalism. That they succeeded is beyond dispute. Yet that very question—the success and even the propriety of government helping those who cannot help themselves—is very much a part of the national debate today.

Whether placed in lofty philosophical terms sanctifying the work ethic or in cruel denigration of the undeserving poor, the controversy remains the same today as it has through the ages. Because they came into the American consciousness at the same time, there are innumerable comparisons between the modern war on poverty and the war in Vietnam. Both cost billions of dollars. Both had an effect on the American economy. Both were hotly debated and remain so today. And neither was "won" by the United States; in both cases, we simply abandoned the field. We tend to forget that there are real people's lives at stake in these discussions, real mothers, real fathers, real children, real grandparents.

If the poor have always been with us in America, we tend to aim our arguments almost entirely at the successes or failures of the last twenty-five years, or at best, the twenty years between Dwight Eisenhower leaving the White House in 1960 and Ronald Reagan entering it in 1980. Not coincidentally, these were also the years of greatest progress in race relations in the twentieth century; and, like the effort aimed at ending poverty, the drive to eliminate apartheid in America began and ended the same way—first in the hearts and minds of the people, then through the actions of the legislatures and presidents they helped elect.

Aggressive, interventionist government became a popularly accepted idea in America only fifty years ago. We eagerly embraced that then-radical notion of course, only because the private economy clearly demonstrated its inability to beat back the depression and put wages into people's pockets once again.

We Americans embraced big government again in the late 1950s, when it became clear there would never be any private sector or state-level commitment to ending racial segregation without federal government intervention. And by 1960 it was equally plain that the capitalist system had failed to moderate or restrain the privation which afflicted one in every five Americans 25 years ago. John E. Schwarz details the problem then:

> Imagine all the people living today in the industrial states of Massachusetts and Michigan, with such cities as Boston and Detroit. Then add all the people living in the states of Minnesota, Colorado,

Oregon, Arizona, Maryland, and Kentucky. These states contain Minneapolis, St. Paul, Denver, Portland, Phoenix, Tucson, Baltimore and Louisville . . . Include some of the more rural states such as New Hampshire, South Carolina, and Iowa. Then imagine every person in every one of these states living in poverty. That describes the number of people and the breadth of poverty existing in America in 1960 at the end of the Eisenhower era.[1]

Remember that being poor then was different; remember too that part of today's debate about fighting poverty is less about how and whether to fight poverty and more about how to define it.

In 1959, poverty was defined by an income of $2,973 or less for a family of four living in an urban area. By 1970, the poverty income level, adjusted for inflation, was $3,970. By 1979, a family earning less than $7,412 qualified as poor. In 1983, the four person family needed $10,178 to escape being poor.

Many of the 1960s poor, it must be remembered, had worked for most of their adult lives, yet the income they generated from forty hours or more of work a week was not sufficient to maintain a family or to lift them above the government's poverty line. With as many as 50 million Americans unable to provide life's basic necessities for themselves, and millions more facing near-poverty, the Kennedy, Johnson and Nixon years saw an enormous expansion of government's efforts to aid the poor.

These efforts fell essentially into three areas. Some gave direct cash assistance, usable by the recipient for any purpose and included the much-maligned Aid to Families With Dependent Children, supplemental income programs for the elderly poor, and Social Security and unemployment compensation.

A second kind of assistance had a more direct aim, particularly toward health and housing. Best known among these programs are Medicare and Medicaid, food stamps, public housing, and rent supplement programs. Finally, a third kind of support was directed toward improving the marketable skills of the poor, enabling them to compete successfully in the private economy.

Although many in the late 1960s suggested that a newly-existing "silent majority" of Americans strongly disapproved of these programs, a wealth of public-opinion data demonstrated that a solid majority supported government programs to end poverty at the beginning of the 1960s and continued to do so even after the programs were underway. Now the Reagan Administration wants to change the description of poverty and thus decrease the number of Americans who need assistance from their government. Using the 1955 definition, 11.7% of the population were poor in 1979 (the year before Ronald Reagan took office). By 1983, 15.2% of all Americans were poor, and the figure is rising. But the Administration wants to compute poverty in one of several new ways, each of which would show a smaller percentage of Americans destitute today and at the same time provide a factual rationale for further domestic cuts.

Counting non-cash benefits—like food and housing—would have meant only 9.7% of the population was poor in 1979 instead of 11.7% and that 13.8%—not 15.2%—are poor today. But any of the nine new methods proposed by the Office of Management and Budget and the Census Bureau demonstrate that poverty in America is pervasive and progressive; there are simply more people poor in America today than there were four years ago.

Including non-cash benefits in measuring poverty requires including them in measuring the status of the non-poor as well. If pension benefits, employee health plans and taxpayer subsidized two-martini lunches are included in measuring the economic status of all American wage-earners, the disparity between the poor and non-poor and the staggering mal-distribution of wealth in America is likely to be far greater than it is under any measure being contemplated today.

Using disposable income as a measure isn't totally reliable either. Since the income tax threshold—the point at which a low-income worker must start paying taxes—has dropped as a result of the shift in the tax burden over the last four years from the rich to the middle classes and the poor, substantial numbers of low-income workers now have even their small incomes eaten away by federal income taxes. As a result of the 1981 tax changes alone, families earning $80,000 or more received tax cuts averaging $8,390 last year; those with incomes under $10,000 lost an average $390.

The Reagan Administration believes that poverty has been nearly eliminated in America and that the only effort required today is maintenance, or safety net protection, for a collection of people who find themselves temporarily untouched by the economic recovery. And, they believe that a reduction in poverty occurred not because of anything government did but in spite of it, and because of the benign effects of the invisible hand of the free market. They claim the growth in wages and salaries and new jobs in the 1960s and '70s as proof of the private economy's ability to heal its own wounds and to care for its own wounded, but in fact the rate of poverty was barely affected by the new affluence.

When income transfers from government programs are subtracted from real income, even in times of sustained government growth, one in every five Americans is still poor. The rising tide doesn't lift all boats, especially old boats, black boats, and female boats. Real, disposable income per person in the United States went up 24% between 1965 and 1972 but, subtracting government income transfers, the percentage of male-headed elderly families living in poverty went down only 6%.

There was no reduction in the number of poverty-level female-headed elderly families. In that same period of rapid economic growth, the number of younger female-headed poor white families increased, when income transfers were discarded. For women under 25 heading families, this period of economic prosperity was devastating without government assistance. Seven years of vigorous growth affected them not one iota.

To say that programs which serve low-income Americans contribute to the deficit is to be irresponsible and foolish. It is elementary arithmetic—perhaps not part of the curriculum in Dixon, Illinois years ago—that when revenues go down and expenses go up, deficits will result. For fiscal 1985 alone, revenues into the federal treasury declined by an estimated $116 billion dollars because of President Reagan's tax law changes. In other words, more than one-half of this year's deficit flows directly from the excessive and inequitable tax cuts of '81 and '82.

Increases in defense spending account for another 25% of the deficit. For fiscal '85, the President proposed a $35 billion increase in defense spending, raising defense outlays to $272 billion dollars, 70% higher than the 1981 spending level. Interest payments, which reflect the increase in federal debt, will go up $8 billion. Thus revenue losses from tax cuts, military spending and higher interest payments will amount to $159 billion dollars, or 82% of the $195 billion fiscal '85 deficit. On the other hand, at President Reagan's urging, congress cut an estimated $75 billion from various social, economic and welfare programs—a contribution to deficit reduction from mothers of dependent children, the school lunch program, and from mothers who want job training.

The most callous argument against government assistance is that it somehow saps the will to work of those who receive it. As usual, the facts suggest something very different. Between 1965 and 1980, our target years, employment in America (the number of people seeking and taking work) increased by 35%. Would this figure have been higher had there been less money spent on welfare programs? One study says had Medicaid, AFDC, food Stamps and veteran's benefits been eliminated, the number of hours worked by Americans would have increased about 1%.[2]

Yet, beginning in 1965 as government anti-poverty programs grew, the rate of unemployment decreased, being less in America than in most other Western nations. The increase in employment and the slow growth rate in unemployment make it clear that government efforts against poverty had little effect on the number of Americans who wanted productive, paying employment.

If so many Americans had jobs, who were the people on welfare? By the end of the 1970s, only 14% of AFDC families were male-headed, and half of these were incapacitated by injury, lung disease, or some other disabling handicap. Of the remainder, most had no skill and less than a high school education but were required by law to participate in a work training program or else lose welfare assistance. From 1960 until 1980, the vast majority of AFDC recipients were mothers of just over two children, widowed or otherwise separated from their children's fathers. Sixty to 75% of AFDC recipients leave the rolls—within three years.[3]

And so, by the end of the 1970s, the war on poverty could claim victory in some significant battles, even if the final victory was still far away. The percentage of Americans living in poverty had declined and food stamp and nutritional programs were effective in reducing malnutrition.

In health care, another revolution had occurred. In 1963, before the establishment of Medicare and Medicaid, fully 20% of the poverty population had never seen a physician. By 1970, that figure had dropped to only 8%. The number of prenatal visits made by poor women to physicians rose dramatically, as did the number of visits to physicians made by poor people in general. Most impressively, from 1965 to 1975, the infant mortality rate among the poor fell by 33%.

In housing, the results are equally impressive. In 1960, 20% of American households lived in substandard housing, by 1976 that figure was only 8%.

Studies of government job training programs have also shown impressive results. A study of Head Start children showed them less likely to be assigned to special education classes than other non-Head Start low income children, less likely to be held back a grade, and demonstrating an immediate 7-point IQ score increase as a result of their participation in the program.

From all the evidence, three conclusions stand out. First, poverty cannot be eliminated simply by full-time hard work, as more than 5 million hard-working poor Americans could testify today. Next, the private sector's growth, however vigorous, cannot be depended upon to reduce poverty more than marginally. And finally, government's efforts, however clumsy and flawed, did succeed. They reduced poverty by more than half and relieved some of poverty's grimmest conditions—malnutrition, poor housing, ill health. They provided successful job training, raising the economic level of thousands of Americans. They provided early education for low-income children, increasing their chance for success in school and the job market.

In spite all of this evidence, the conclusion of most Americans today would be that these programs were absolute failures, that they helped create a massive, cumbersome government whose excessive taxes and bureaucracy, burdensome rules and regulations had strangled our national will. None of this is true. Taxes, as a percentage of income, were little higher in the '60s and '70s than they were in the '50s. Bureaucracy, in proportion to the employed work force, rose only marginally after 1960. The rate of business investment continued as strongly in the '60s and '70s as in the '50s, when it was unhampered by stringent regulation.

But other forces acted to change facts to fiction and fiction to fact. American business invested huge sums in daily argument against regulation and big government, in advertisements, through support for anti-big government candidates, and through the establishment of pseudo-academic institutions which provided an intellectual rationalization for smaller, less intrusive government. Liberals helped this assault on public opinion by having almost no coherent opinions of their own, except a marked reluctance to defend the programs and style of government they helped create.

The election in 1980 began the process of dismantling the war on poverty, with disastrous results for America's poor. Government programs serving the poor were cut twice as deeply (in proportionate terms) as other programs. One million food stamp recipients lost their benefits, and the average benefit was reduced to $.47 per person per meal. 500,000 low income working families lost AFDC benefits. 700,000 children lost Medicaid coverage, leaving 3 of every 10 children living in poverty without Medicaid coverage. All four million residents of public housing had their rents raised. Low income housing funds have been cut by two-thirds, forcing 300,000 more families into sub-standard housing by the end of this year. Three-hundred and seventy-five legal services offices have been closed, and the number of attorneys and paralegals providing services has dropped by 30%. Four-hundred and forty-thousand children have lost compensatory education services. Two-hundred and thirty-nine community health centers have had to curtail their services, and 725,000 people, most of them children, have lost access to health care at neighborhood centers. Five-hundred thousand children have been pushed off the school lunch line. One-hundred and fifty-thousand low income families have lost day care services. After reductions in aid for low and moderate income students, the numbers of black high school graduates going to college fell 36%.

For most black people, the last four years have been cataclysmic and for some fatal. The Urban Institute reports that the average middle class black family had a lower standard of living in 1984 than in 1980, just as the average poor black family did. Hardest hit were two-parent families with one parent working and the other managing the home and children—these families suffered an average loss of $2000 apiece in disposable income. More black Americans lived in poverty in 1983—9.9 million—than in any year since the Census Bureau began collecting data on black poverty twenty years ago. After twenty years of decline, the infant mortality rate of black Americans has started to increase.

If one mark of the success of a society is how it cares for the helpless, the last four years have been an American failure. The future promises little better. Whether viewed as a mandate for President Reagan's policies or an endorsement of his personality, the 1984 election results were dramatic.

Exit polls and other surveys taken both before and after the election show dangerous racial and class stratifications in the American electorate. They also promise hard times ahead for those who found themselves on the losing side. But if the years that went before, the Kennedy, Johnson and Carter years, taught us any lesson at all, it was that government, under militant and concerted pressure, would move, all too often with deliberate lack of speed, to become a limited partner of sorts with the American underclass in their struggle to do better for themselves. If we are to believe with

Thomas Jefferson that the common man is "the most precious portion of the state," we find that resource in danger of economic extinction today. Human problems are now placed on a balance sheet, forced to add up, to pay profit for themselves.

There can be no better prescription for relieving this crisis and for reviving some real interest in it than to recreate the same non-partisan national coalition of conscience that helped create the New Deal, Great Society and New Frontier. What is so frightening about diminished life chances for black and poor Americans is not just that so many of our fellow citizens are not aware, but that many are aware and simply do not care. Creating that care, and protecting the fragile structures whittled away over the last four years is first priority for today. How is that done?

First by immersing ourselves in politics, both in the narrow, partisan definition of that art, and in larger definition which includes the shaping of every relationship between people and the institutions, both public and private, which affect and control their lives. Fairness, growth, full employment, economic democracy—these are the issues upon which yesterday's defeated can become tomorrow's victors. Roosevelt, Truman, Kennedy—the candidate who summoned up their memory triumphed. For defeated Democrats to believe they can succeed by turning their backs on their principles, and by turning away from their most loyal supporters, is a clear misreading of the Reagan landslide. Building such a movement is difficult but not impossible. Surely every one of us wants to have a say in deciding our common fate.

One beneficial result of yesterday's people's movements is the proliferation of progressive interest organizations, representing those for whom almost no one spoke just twenty short years ago. These groups work well together on the national level in setting a progressive political agenda; they have failed, however, to develop local level solidarity at the grass roots or to lead their membership to work together as closely as their leadership does.

There is a massive army of angry, dissatisfied and dispossessed Americans, robbed of their fair share of the national treasure. Once mobilized, they will be invincible, but they must be organized, educated, and agitated to see their common interest more clearly in the future than they have done in the past.

For only a little more than twenty years has this nation had a half-hearted commitment to end the causes and effects of the deification of a system of economics which depends on exploitation for its existence. After twenty years of minimum effort aimed at undoing nearly 200 years of putting profit before people, we are now told that the effort has been a failure and that it has hurt the people who are beneficiaries of 200 years of economic exploitation. We have a world to win, if we will.

Notes

[1]John E. Schwarz, *America's Hidden Success—A Reassessment of Twenty Years of Public Policy* (New York: W.W. Norton and Company, 1983).

[2]Shelton Danziger *et al.*, "How Income Transfer Programs Affect Work, Savings, and Income Distribution: A Critical Review." *Journal of Economic Literature*, September 1984, p. 996, Table 7.

[3]Sar A. Levitan, *Programs in Aid of the Poor* (Baltimore: The Johns Hopkins University Press, 1976), pp. 34-35. Also, United States Bureau of the Census, SAUS; 1980, p. 358, Table 577.

POVERTY AND
THE PLIGHT OF THE FARM WORKER

by César Chávez

Twenty-one years ago last September, on a lonely stretch of railroad track paralleling U.S. Highway 101 near Salinas, 32 bracero farm workers lost their lives in a tragic accident. The braceros had been imported from Mexico to work on California farms. They died when their bus, a converted flatbed truck, drove in front of a freight train. Conversion of the bus had not been approved by any government agency. The driver had tunnel vision. Most of the bodies lay unidentified for days. No one, including the grower who employed the workers, knew their names.

The circumstances surrounding this tragedy are not uncommon in the lives of farm workers. Today, thousands of farm workers live under savage conditions—beneath trees and amid garbage and human excrement, near tomato fields in San Diego County (tomato fields on which the most modern farm technology is used). Vicious rats gnaw on the workers as they sleep. Workers walk miles to buy food at inflated prices and carry water in from irrigation ditches.

Child labor is still common in these areas. Under-age children account for nearly 30 percent of Northern California's garlic harvesters. Some 800,000 under-age children work with harvesting crops across America. Because they qualify as workers, kids as young as six years old have voted in state-conducted union elections. Babies born to migrant workers face an infant mortality rate 25 percent higher that that of the rest of the population, and a malnutrition rate ten times higher than the national rate. The farm workers' average life expectancy is 49 years, compared to 73 years for the average non-migrant American.

All my life, I have been driven by one dream, one goal, one vision: to overthrow a farm labor system in this nation that treats farm workers as if they were not human, as if they were agricultural implements or beasts of burden simply to be used and discarded. This dream was born in my youth. It was nurtured in my early days of organizing. It has flourished and it has been attacked.

This dream, this vision grew as I watched what my mother and father went through, what we experienced as migrant farm workers in California. It grew with the desire to be treated fairly; it grew with anger and rage—emotions I felt 40 years ago when people of my color were denied the right to see a movie or eat at a restaurant; it grew from the frustration and humiliation I felt as a boy who couldn't understand how the growers could abuse and exploit farm workers when there were so many of us and so few of them.

In the 50s, in San Jose, Los Angeles, and other urban communities, we—the Mexican American people—were dominated by an Anglo majority. I soon realized what other minority people had discovered: that the only answer, the only hope, was in organizing. More of us had to become citizens. We had to register to vote. And people like me had to develop the skills it would take to organize, to educate, to help empower the Chicano people.

I spent many years before we founded the union learning how to work with people. We experienced some success in voter registration and in battling racial discrimination—successes at a time when Black Americans were just beginning to assert their civil rights and when Hispanics were virtually unaware of theirs. But deep in my heart I knew I could never be happy unless I tried organizing the farm workers. I didn't know if I would succeed, but I had to try.

All Hispanics, urban and rural, young and old, were connected to the farm worker's experience. We had all lived through the fields, or our parents had; we shared that common humiliation. How could we progress as a people, even if we lived in the cities, while the farm workers were condemned to a life, in the fields, without pride? How could our people believe that their children could become lawyers and doctors and judges and business people while this shame, this injustice continued?

Those who attack our union often say, "It's not really a union. It's something else, a social movement, a civil rights movement. It's something dangerous." They're half right. The United Farm Workers is first and foremost a union, but it is something more.

In the beginning, the UFW attacked the source of shame with

which our people lived. We attacked injustice and poor living conditions, not by complaining, not by seeking hand-outs, not by becoming soldiers in the War on Poverty, but by organizing. Acknowledging that we had allowed ourselves to become victims in a democratic society, a society where majority rule and collective bargaining are supposed to be more than academic theories or political rhetoric, we acquired confidence and pride and hope.

As the UFW became visible, Chicanos started entering college in greater numbers, Hispanics began running for public office, our people started asserting their rights on a broad range of issues. The union's survival—its very existence—told Hispanics we were fighting for our dignity, challenging and overcoming injustice, and empowering the least educated and the poorest among us. The message was clear: if it could happen in the fields, it could happen anywhere—in cities, courts, councils, and state legislatures.

I didn't really appreciate it at the time, but the coming of our union signaled the start of great changes among Hispanics. I've travelled to every part of this nation, spoken with thousands of Hispanics from every walk of life, and most have told me the farm workers filled them with hope and inspiration.

Although our opponents declare the union weak, saying it has not grown fast enough and that even farm workers themselves no longer support it, research has proven otherwise. Researchers in the Department of Anthropology at Purdue University have found that farm workers view the farm labor movement, particularly the United Farm Workers of America, as the best opportunity to improve their lives. W. Kenneth Barger, Chairman of the Department of Anthropology at the University, and director of the study, indicated that until now, farm workers' views about the farm labor movement in general and the UFW in particular have not been adequately documented.

A point now documented by the study is that California farm workers endorse the United Farm Workers of America and believe the UFW offers the best alternative for improving their lives. Ninety-one percent of the grape workers surveyed in the lower San Joaquin Valley believe the UFW is good for farm workers, and 83 percent think the union's efforts and activities have improved the lives of farm laborers.

The survey found that farm workers covered by UFW collective bargaining agreements expressed more satisfaction with work benefits, felt a greater sense of job security, and felt they had greater access to health care than non-union workers. UFW workers also indicated greater stability in such areas as marital status, owning homes, and in bilingual literacy. So it seems ironic that the same forces that so passionately claim the union is not influential, are the same forces that fight us so hard.

Although they claim we are weak and unsuccessful, growers continue to fight us because our very existence forces them to spend millions year after year on increased wages, improved working conditions, and benefits for *all* workers, even those not working under union contract.

It doesn't really matter whether we have 100,000 members or 500,000 members. In truth, hundreds of thousands of farm workers in California and in other states are better off today because of our work. Hispanics across California and the nation who don't work in agriculture, are better off today because of what the farm workers have taught: organization, pride, strength, seizing control over one's own life. Tens of thousands of the children and grandchildren of poor Hispanics are moving out of the fields and barrios and into business and politics. At companies where farm workers are protected by union contracts, we have made progress in overcoming such evils as child labor, low wages, poor working conditions, sexual harassment, discrimination, and crops tainted with pesticides.

But injustices continue and we must remain organized. Thirty-six thousand farm workers who voted to be represented by the UFW in free elections are still waiting for contracts from growers who refuse to bargain in good faith. This may mean that, for farm workers, poverty and all that accompanies it—child labor, infant mortality, malnutrition, short life expectancy, inhuman living and working conditions—will continue.

Is this a make-believe threat? Ask the family of René López, the young farm worker in Fresno who was shot to death last year because he supported the union. Ask the farm workers who watch as their children go hungry in this land of wealth and promise. Ask the farm workers who see their lives eaten away by poverty and suffering. (These tragic events forced farm workers to declare a new international boycott of all California table grapes except the 30 percent produced under UFW contract.)

In the past, our boycotts have been successful and they are now even more so. We have achieved more success in the first 11 months of 1984 than in the 14 years since 1970. But we have another source of hope for our cause—the monumental growth of Hispanic influence in this country. That means for us increased population, increased social and economic clout, and increased political influence.

South of the Sacramento River, Hispanics now make up more than 25 percent of the population. That figure will top 30 percent by the year 2000. There are 1.1 million Spanish-surnamed registered voters in California. In 1975, there were 200 Hispanic elected officials at all levels of government. In 1984, there are over 400 elected judges, city council members, mayors, and legislators. In light of these trends, it is absurd to believe or suggest that we are going to go back in time, as a union or as a people.

I am told these days why farm workers should be discouraged and pessimistic: the Republicans control the Governor's office and the White House; there is a conservative trend in the nation. Yet we are filled with hope and encouragement. We have looked into the future and the future is ours. The farm workers and their children—and the Hispanics and their children—are the future in California. Those politicians who ally themselves with the corporate growers and against the farm workers and the Hispanics, are in for a big surprise. They want to make their careers in politics; they want to hold power 20 and 30 years from now. But in 20 and 30 years from now Modesto, Salinas, Fresno, Bakersfield, the Imperial Valley, and many of the great cities of California will be dominated by farm workers, by the children and grandchildren of farm workers, not by growers.

These trends are part of the forces of history which cannot be stopped. No person and no organization can resist them for very long; they are inevitable. Once social change begins, it cannot be reversed. You cannot uneducate the person who has learned to read, nor humiliate the person who feels pride, nor oppress the people who are not afraid any more.

Our opponents must understand that it is not just a union we have built. Unions, like other institutions, come and go. But for nearly 20 years, our union has been on the cutting edge of a people's cause and you cannot do away with an entire people. Regardless of what the future holds for the unions, regardless of what the future holds for farm workers, our accomplishments cannot be undone. "La Causa" doesn't have to be experienced twice. The consciousness and pride that were raised by our union are alive and thriving inside millions of young Hispanics who will never work on a farm.

Like the other immigrant groups, the day will come when we win the economic, political, and social benefits which are in keeping with both our numbers in society and our dignity. The day will come when the politicians will do the right thing by our people out of political necessity and not out of charity or idealism. The day will come when we will be treated not as objects of charity or mere tools of production, but as a people who have organized ourselves and have eradicated the causes underlying the injustices and poverty inflicted upon us.

REAGANOMICS, WOMEN, AND POVERTY

Sharon N. Skog

In case you hadn't noticed, the poor—the once-invisible, the "other" Americans—are making headlines these days. A not infrequent story on the network news—especially during the frigid winter months—concerns the homeless. Politicians bandy about such little understood terms as "feminization of poverty" and "comparable worth" when discussing major issues of our time and mouthing promises to attract supporters. Even cartoonists such as Tom Toles of the *Buffalo News* and Garry Trudeau of "Doonesbury" fame address the plight of the poor, mostly by taking potshots at the Reagan Administration's attitude toward and approach to poverty.

For example, in a recent editorial page cartoon entitled "Psychic Predictions for 1985," Tom Toles created six scenarios about the future political and economic climate in this country, including one which touched on the issue of poverty. Each of the six frames was constructed in a multiple choice fashion. Frame 5 stated:

The one war the administration is sure to *avoid* in 1985 is the war:

A. in Central America
B. in the Middle East
C. on poverty

Choice "C" was circled.[1]

Gary Trudeau of "Doonesbury" also took some swipes at the Reagan Administration on the issue of poverty in a holiday series on the homeless. Rick put in a call to the White House as a desperate last appeal to find a missing homeless woman who, unbeknown to him, was buried under a blanket of snow on a park bench outside 1600 Pennsylvania Avenue. The responses Rick got to his inquiries about the missing woman were as follows:

W.H.: I'm afraid no one's here, sir. Everyone's on vacation. Have
   you tried the D.C. police?
Rick: Of course, I've tried the D.C. police! And the park police! And
   the mayor's office! No one has time to look for a missing
   homeless woman!
W.H.: I'm afraid there isn't anything I can do, sir.
Rick: Dammit! Doesn't anyone care about what happens to these
   people?
W.H.: I'm sorry sir. It's really not our responsibility.[2]

Why all the hoopla *now* about the poor who, as some would
argue, have always been and will always be with us? There are, I
believe, a number of reasons for this increased visibility, including:

1. the rise of a new class of poor people, referred to as the "new
   poor;" that is, a change in the composition of the poverty
   population;
2. the growing chasm between the "haves" and "have nots" in
   this society;
3. the insensitivity—indeed, the cynicism and meanness—of
   the Reagan Administration toward the poor.

Among the "new poor" hardest hit—those whose numbers are
increasing exponentially on an annual basis; those who are prime
targets of the scalpel of the Reagan Administration—are women
and children. It is on this group of the poverty population—primarily poor working mothers and recipients of Aid to Families with
Dependent Children (AFDC)—the phenomenon of "feminization
of poverty," and the effects of Reaganomics on poor women and
children that I shall focus my attention. In this essay I shall *not*
address in any specific manner the special problems and needs of
midlife and older women or the additional burden of race discrimination that minority women encounter.

In order to place in proper perspective the events and trends of
the past 20 years, which have led to the increased impoverishment
of women and their children, it is important to examine some deep-
seated traditions and attitudes about women—their role and status—that have prevailed throughout this country's history. In con-
sidering American women's social, economic, and legal legacy, we
will, I trust, better comprehend women's current predicament.

Women's poverty is not simply a function of the recent changes
in America's economic and social fabric. Rather, the feminization of
poverty—and its presaged continuation—is rooted in customs and

laws that historically and systematically have discriminated against women and have set women apart in an inferior class. Further, Reaganomics has served to exacerbate women's plight and perpetuate the feminization of poverty. To better understand and evaluate the effects of Reaganomics on poor women and children, we shall look at the underlying values and assumptions of that philosophy and their embodiment in recent policy decisions.

There is nothing particularly new about the fact that there are poor women and children in the United States. Hence, the Reagan Administration alone is not to blame for the plight of poor women and children. What *is* new is that women, by virtue of present-day social and economic processes, are increasingly bearing the brunt of being poor in America. According to the National Advisory Council on Economic Opportunity:

> All other things being equal, if the proportion of the poor in female-householder families were to continue to increase at the same rate as it did from 1967 to 1978, the poverty population would be composed solely of women and children before the year 2000.[3]

Although poverty in America declined from 1960 to 1978 as a result of the War on Poverty and the anti-poverty programs that were established, poverty among women as a proportion of poverty among all groups rose during the same time. What conditions gave rise to this phenomenon? This alarming trend—identified as the "feminization of poverty"—can be explained in terms of a number of significant social and economic changes in the lives of American women during the past 20 years. Such changes which have contributed, in part, to the rising impoverishment of women are the increase in the number of female-headed households, the recent economic recession which left many—women and men alike—unemployed, and cuts in social welfare programs.

In addition to these recent social and economic trends, there are several other factors steeped in tradition and reflective of conventional "wisdom" about women and women's role which have provided the foundation for the current trend of increasing poverty among women and children. These contributing factors, which we will examine, pertain to women's second-class citizenship—i.e., their inferior social and legal status, job segregation, wage disparity and discrimination, non-enforcement of child support orders (private assistance), inadequate AFDC support (public assistance), and lack of affordable child care.

With the rise in the rates of separation, divorce, and single women and teenage pregnancies, there have been significant changes in the American family structure and the number of households headed by women has increased dramatically in the last 20 years. As more households have been headed by women, families have become more at risk of sinking into poverty. In 1981, a child living in a female-headed household was five to six times more likely to be living in poverty than one residing in a male-headed household. Although only one in five households is maintained by women (12% of white families and 40% of black families), single mothers constitute the fastest growing *poverty* population in the United States today. More than 50% of all *poor* families are headed by women. In California, in 1984, 64% of all female-headed households (or 1.5 million women and children) were supported by AFDC. But 25% of all poor American children live in homes headed by women who work *full-time*.

Upon further investigation of the facts, what do these shocking statistics reveal? In short:

1. Women *alone* frequently do not have the economic capability to adequately provide for a family. Many women, whether working full-time in the labor force or receiving public assistance, are not able to make financial ends meet.

2. Those women who are in the labor force—46 million total and 40.5% of the labor force in October 1984—are generally concentrated in low-paying, "pink ghetto" or female-dominated (and therefore undervalued) occupations in low-paying industries. Despite the fact that women have increased their participation in the labor force and contribution to the family income, they have suffered economically as a result of job segregation and wage discrimination.

3. Women's standard of living is lowered substantially while that of men increases markedly following divorce, in large measure, because absent fathers fail and are not compelled to provide child support and thus shift the economic as well as other responsibilities solely on to women. This constitutes an extreme burden for women who continue to assume primary childrearing responsibilities and are the least able to provide adequate economic support due to their limited access to well-paid work.

4. Because of their childrearing responsibilities and given the lack of support and accommodation in the workplace to sin-

gle parents' needs, many women, if part of the labor force, hold part-time or marginal jobs which are low-paying and without important benefits such as health insurance.

5. Women who work outside the home spend a considerable portion of their earnings on child care, thus making it difficult to meet other living expenses.

6. Given these circumstances, many women are forced to make difficult choices. They are often required to decide whether to work in the labor force for low pay and leave their children in the care of another or dispense with child care altogether if unavailable and/or unaffordable; *or* suffer intimidation and the humiliation of being a welfare recipient in order to have financial support and benefits which are greater than what can be acquired through wage labor.

It is clear from this brief outline of the facts that, currently, women and their families are vulnerable economically for a host of reasons which are traceable to historic views about women and their role in society. Such vulnerabilities of women and their predicament are well-depicted and summarized by one welfare mother who testified in a recent California Feminization of Poverty hearing:

> For 13 years of marriage, I remained primarily in the home and took for granted the amenities of our American way of life—the right to privacy, access to opportunity, and prosperity. Now, I've found myself alone with five children ages 3 through 10, no marketable skills, no social support, and inadequate economic support. I was stripped of the social status that had been conferred on me through marriage. In contrast, although my spouse had deprived himself of his family by leaving the state, his work experience and standard of living remained intact. For me, the very process of applying for aid was a symbolic stripping of my integrity and self-esteem . . . this would not have been necessary had my former spouse paid support or if the system could have compelled him to do so.[4]

The feelings and grave problems that this mother conveys are clear enough, but may be explained and possibly better understood in terms of the legacy American women have inherited. Historically, women in this country have been classified as second-class citizens and subjected to sex discrimination in all of its many forms. Their demeaned social and legal status has been traditionally prescribed as a result of long-accepted notions about their biological nature and function. Regarded as the physically delicate and weaker, "fairer" sex and thus, physically inferior, women have been the subject of protective legislation, originally considered salutary, but now viewed by many as discriminatory in effect. They have been excluded from occupations thought to be too strenuous and potentially damaging to future mothers and children, and they have been denied opportunities for upward mobility in the labor market comparable to those available for men.

Not only have women been classified as *physically* inferior, but they have been deemed *mentally* inferior and therefore incapable of performing social roles outside the institutions of marriage and family. Hence, women typically have been highly discouraged from succeeding academically and pursuing professional careers. Instead, they have been encouraged to fulfill their biological function as mothers, demonstrate competency as wives, mothers, and homemakers, and depend on men for occupational prestige, financial support, and decision-making.

Historically, belief in the myths that women are physically and mentally inferior to men has fostered acceptance of the idea that men and women are inherently unequal. That men and women are unequal has, until recently, been inculcated as a matter of fact, as well as a social ideal. Naturally, the transmission of such an ideal from generation to generation has had significant repercussions. The socialization process and the legal system in this country have been tremendously affected. A singular biological function—childbearing—has served as the foundation for determining all social roles and legal status. Because of women's unique capacity for childbearing, their socially prescribed functions in life have been family-centered. However, women have sacrificed and suffered much as a result of such circumscription. In preparation for a domestic role, young girls have often bypassed opportunities to excel in other generally, more highly valued pursuits and in the role of wife-mother-homemaker, women have had little time and encouragement to express themselves in other than a domestic setting. The consequences of these circumstances have been varied, but largely devastating in nature. Due to a lack of education and training for occupations in the work force which might enable women to be independent and given the undervaluation of "women's work," women have been left psychologically and economically dependent, and often, unfulfilled as human beings. Denied choices and opportunities comparable to those afforded men in this society, women have been relegated to second-class status both as a matter of convention and law and have been ill-prepared and ill-equipped to face the challenges and responsibilities brought on by the social changes of the last 20 years.

Since the 1960s with the persistent, driving force of the women's movement, there has been a continuous attack on the myths and presuppositions about women's role and a slow dismantling of the structures which have fostered sexual inequality in the United States. Many new laws have been instituted which counter the "old wisdom" and instead, recognize and call for equality of the sexes, thus making it more possible for women to exercise tenable choices and greater control of their own lives. However, despite the considerable strides made in the past 25 years, women continue to suffer from discrimination as a consequence of job segregation, wage disparity, and lack of adequate support systems such as child support and affordable child care. Thus, in reality, women continue to face obstacles in their efforts to be independent and many find themselves in a dependent, and therefore, weak and inferior position.

Female heads of household who lack marketable skills and/or are unable to find adequate-paying jobs are frequently dependent on AFDC to support themselves and their children. Contrary to popular perception about welfare recipients as lazy freeloaders (a perception that is rampant in the Reagan Administration), these women *need* and *want* to work. But for many reasons pertaining to women's role and the nature of the marketplace, which were discussed earlier, these women are caught in a vicious cycle of dependence—first, dependence usually on a husband and then, following dissolution of the marriage and the husband's failure to provide adequate, if any, child support, dependence, at least for a time, on welfare.

In marriage and out, mothers today who do not have good-paying jobs are at the mercy of others for subsistence support—either private or public assistance. Neither amounts to adequate support. In the case of private child support, the average annual award in 1980 was $2050; the amount actually paid was $1120—hardly sufficient to meet even the day care, not to mention other living costs for children of working mothers. In the case of public assistance or AFDC, a family of three in California received $526 per month in 1984. This is approximately 43% of the median estimate made by Americans in 1984 who thought that it takes a minimum of $300 per week for a non-farm family of three or four to get by. No wonder then that women and children who are welfare recipients in this country are barely surviving and often have nothing to eat at the end of the month when the AFDC payment cannot be stretched any further.

Yet, since 1981, the Reagan Administration, in the process of implementing Reaganomics, has swung a mighty axe to many social programs which have benefited, in the immediate and longer term, the welfare and working poor. In so doing, the Administration has signaled to the poor—to women and children—in America that their problems are not government's or society's but rather their own to solve. This attitude reflects not only a lack of compassion but also a complete denial of the facts and blindness to the conditions which have led to increased poverty in the United States.

In order to glean some insight into the Reagan Administration's rationale for cutting social programs so vital to poor women and children, we need to assess Reaganomics in terms of its underlying values and assumptions and its embodiment in policies that affect poor women and their children.

"Reaganomics," now quite commonplace in our vocabulary, denotes a philosophy of economics, government, and welfare that, from the point of view of the poverty population in the United States, mirrors an attitude of disdain. It is an ideology which is mired in a conservative tradition blind to the new realities of the '80s and years to come. Reaganomics denounces the liberal, humanitarian values that were prevalent in the '60s and '70s and embodied in many social programs and policies of that bygone era. In stark contrast to the more benevolent spirit, heightened social consciousness, and longer-ranged, visionary orientation of the previous 20 pre-Reagan years, the Reagan years are characterized by parsimony, acute myopia, flagrant disregard for the disadvantaged in our society, and excessive attention to profitability—when it seems appropriate.

Reaganomics is founded on conventional "wisdom" about the marketplace and government's role vis a vis that arena and evokes such traditions as *laissez faire* economic theory and Darwinian notions about survival. The clarion message of this philosophy is, "God helps those who help themselves." Individualism—rather than social awareness and responsibility—is paramount.

Practically speaking, applied Reaganomics is evidenced in federal budget cuts of several anti-poverty and social programs and in tax breaks and incentives for the most advantaged—i.e., for 2% of all American households, or those which have incomes of $80,000 and more. Federalism has been restored and reinterpreted. Labeled "new federalism," it has called for a shift in responsibility from the federal to state and local governments where provision for social programs, including AFDC, are concerned. This new conception of federalism has conveniently shrouded the Administration's abnegation of commitment and responsibility to eliminate poverty. The trickle-down theory has assumed new prominence but has gone awry in the translation phase. Job opportunities which were to result from monies available from tax breaks to corporate America have not materialized. However, corporate mergers have increased dramatically. So, the poor, who were to be helped by Reaganomics through private sector initiatives, including the creation of new jobs, have been left out in the cold, in worse straits than before.

According to a 1984 Congressional Budget Office report, the wealthiest in the land have, at least in the short term, reaped considerable benefits from program reductions and tax breaks while the federal deficit has registered ever higher and the poor have been deeply hurt in more, untold ways than we can even measure at this time. Hence, Reaganomics has resurrected and given credence to the adage, "The rich get richer." The rich *have* gotten richer; the poor have gotten poorer; and the already substantial gap between the "haves" and "have nots" in the United States has widened.

Despite publicized facts about the rise in poverty, the emergence of a "new poor" class, as well as an "underclass," and the feminization of poverty in the United States, there are those—and there are many, including leaders in the Reagan Administration—who defy such facts by countering with half-truths. The ultimate effect of so doing is the perpetration of a distorted portrayal of reality which serves to undermine or underestimate the gravity of the problem and effectively ridicule the poor, many of whom are women and their children.

Today, more than half of all women are working outside the home in the paid labor force, and there are more opportunities than ever before for women's advancement in the marketplace. True though these facts are, they do not by themselves convey the complete story about the status of the vast majority of women in the labor force. Nor do such facts lead one to other important truths such as the following:

1. Women in the labor force are earning less than men—$.59-.63 for every $1.00 earned by men—and according to one recent study, were lagging further behind the wages of comparable men in 1980 than they were in 1970, despite the growth of affirmative action and education gains by women during that period.
2. Women on the job are subject to many forms of sex discrimination, the most extreme of which is sexual harassment. Other manifestations of sex discrimination include wage and health benefits discrimination, to mention a couple.
3. Two out of three poor adults in America are women. More women are sinking into poverty and forced to go on welfare because they lack the economic means to support themselves and their children.

The Reagan Administration is guilty of promoting gross misrepresentations of the truth where women's status is concerned. Quick to cite key Cabinet-level appointments of Elizabeth Dole, Margaret Heckler, and Jean Kirkpatrick, as well as the appointment of Sandra Day O'Connor, the first woman Supreme Court Justice, Reagan and his cohorts have been self-congratulatory about the strides they have orchestrated on behalf of women, thus flying in the face of their otherwise abysmal record. It should not be forgotten that this Administration has, in extremely significant ways, thwarted progress toward independence for most American women through non-enforcement and deleterious reinterpretation of such critical laws as the Civil Rights Act of 1964 and the 1972 abortion decision, *Roe v. Wade*.

Similarly, the Reagan Administration has belittled the tragic plight of the poor. Indeed, not only has it underestimated the gravity and pervasiveness of the problem, but even more invidious, the Administration has reviled the poor and then swung the final leveling blow by eviscerating or eliminating federally funded programs vital to the subsistence and welfare of the poor. Unlike the leadership of previous decades, the Reagan Administration has *no* commitment to eradicating poverty. Instead, primacy is given to "objective" market force processes and profitability, among other things.

Since his days as governor of California, Reagan has steadfastly adhered to a standard which focuses on immediate costs and benefits and essentially ignores the long term consequences of budget cuts and policy changes. Now, one of the greatest challenges Reagan as chief economist is facing in the national arena is reduction of the multi-billion dollar, runaway deficit that we have in this country. There is bipartisan consensus among our nation's leadership that the deficit must be cut. The controversy centers upon how to resolve this looming problem. "Raise taxes." "Don't raise taxes." "Cut spending." Defense spending? Social programs?

The Reagan Administration has continuously proposed and implemented budget cuts of social programs while concomitantly advocating and effectuating significant growth in funding for defense. Earlier this year [1985], a draft administration document of the President's fiscal 1986 budget proposed the elimination of such programs as the Small Business Administration and Job Corps and the demise of subsidized school lunches for children from families with incomes over 135% of the poverty line (i.e., families with incomes of $14,220 or more per year). The program eliminations, it was estimated, would constitute a $14 billion (a relatively minor) reduction in the $230 billion deficit. At the same time that such programs, which benefit women, their children, and others who are poor, were being expunged, the Administration was requesting a $33.2 billion *increase* in the military budget for 1986 and projected that, by 1990, the defense budget should mount to $418.3 billion or 35% of total spending for that year. (Currently, this category represents 26% of total budget outlays.) In addition, the proposed budget called for a substantial *reduction*—not simply a freeze on the rate of increase—in spending at eight of the thirteen Cabinet departments, including Agriculture, Education, and Housing and Urban Development.

There are several conclusions that can be drawn from this cursory look at the 1986 deficit reduction scheme. The Administration is making overtures to cut the deficit—a positive step, we might all concede—but as outlined, suggested cuts are being executed in a wholly unsatisfactory way. Even staunch Republican supporters of the President have felt compelled to criticize the Administration's deficit reduction efforts because of their inherently blatant inequities. The deficit is once again being reduced at the expense of the least advantaged in this society—by cutting federal support for and thereby decimating social programs such as school lunches, Medicaid, and subsidized housing. A House Ways and Means Committee study has shown that as a result of 1982 tax and spending cuts at the federal level—which disproportionately penalized poor families—approximately one-half of AFDC recipients lost *all* benefits while another one-quarter lost some benefits. In all, $35.2 billion of aid allocated for social programs were eliminated from the federal budget.

This administration is systematically dismantling anti-poverty programs which, despite whatever their pitfalls, have been necessary safety nets for millions of poor people—among them, women and children—in this country. However, from the Reagan Administration's perspective, such programs are not necessary, helpful, or successful. Rather, this administration believes that most social programs are not cost-effective—or in more blunt terms, are a waste of taxpayer's hard-earned monies. Therefore, it is not surprising that the vise on the poor has been tightened.

Further, a double standard, which is a hallmark of Reaganomics, is manifest. What logic applies insofar as slashing the deficit and social programs are concerned does not apply in the case of the Pentagon budget. This perverse logic is a function of both perception and philosophy. However, if one believes, for example, as do Ed Meese and others in the Reagan Administration, that there are no hungry people in America and that the Communist threat looms large, thereby threatening our national security, then it is entirely comprehensible—albeit, in my estimation, reprehensible—why the proposed 1986 budget proffers *reductions* in social programs and departmental budgets that benefit the poor and *boosts* the military budget, especially for such plans as those to forge ahead with the "Star Wars" missile defense system and to pursue military construction. This proposal is completely consistent with the Reagan Administration's philosophy about the role of the federal government, its attitude toward the poor, and its obsession with national security and military (weapons) superiority. But as Anthony Lewis noted in a 1983 editorial on Reagan budget cuts, such a philosophy suffers from, among other things, defining national security in a very limited way—that is, "as if the security of the United States lay only in weapons and not in the well-being of its people."[5]

The Administration vociferously advertises lower inflation, a rise in the GNP, and a decline in the unemployment rate to the "inflation tolerable" level of 7%. However, whatever one might say about the salutary results of Reaganomics, the critical question is, "At what price?" I would argue that the price is extremely dear when, at a minimum, 35 million or 15% of the American population is essentially disenfranchised—living on the brink with little hope for the future. Ultimately, how we choose to resolve such vexatious problems as poverty is an indication of our values, attitudes, and priorities. The policies and practices we establish are a measure of our commitment—or the lack thereof—to meeting the needs of Americans.

We like to view ourselves as a compassionate people who fight strenuously for democratic principles of liberty and equality. But as we have shifted our national priorities from "quality of life" and civil rights issues to aggregate economic and national security issues, we have, I believe, lost sight of the importance of the cherished democratic ideals of liberty and equality and the need to make it possible for *all* Americans—not just a few—to know the benefits of living in this country. Therefore, I believe, it is incumbent upon us, both in the public and private sectors, and to the benefit of us all to seek creative solutions to our problems. To abate the mounting tide of the feminization of poverty and finally eliminate poverty, we must, at the very least, do the following:

1. reassess our current assumptions about "women's work" and recognize the value and legitimacy of forms of work other than wage labor, including the care and nurturing of children;
2. eradicate all forms of sex discrimination in all arenas, most especially in the labor force;
3. bring an end to job segregation—increase job training opportunities for women workers, expanding opportunities for women in male-dominated occupations;
4. abolish wage and benefits discrimination—institute and enforce comparable worth legislation to promote the concept of "equal pay for work of equal value"; eliminate wage disparity between male and female workers in comparable positions;
5. routinely implement flex time and job sharing opportunities in the workplace;
6. provide quality, affordable child care through a coordinated public/private sector policy;
7. develop child support award formulas at the state level and enforce child support laws;
8. enforce affirmative action legislation at state and federal levels;
9. expand educational opportunities for women, strongly en-

courage them to realize their full potential, and strictly
enforce Title IX of the 1972 Education Amendments;
10. establish grassroots organizations committed to eradicating
poverty in all its various aspects and encourage women to
participate actively in the political process in order to realize these necessary policy changes.

Only when we have instituted these kinds of far-reaching, essential changes will we make it possible for *all* Americans—not just a
few—to know the benefits of living in this country.

Notes

[1]*San Jose Mercury News*, 9 January 1985, n. pag.

[2]*San Jose Mercury News*, 3 January 1985, n. pag.

[3]*Fiscal Report—The American Promise: Equal Justice and Economic Opportunity* (Washington, D.C.: National Advisory Council, 1981), p. 46.

[4]Marsha Nolfi, *Report from Lt. Governor Leo McCarthy's Task Force on the Feminization of Poverty* (January 1985), p. 47.

[5]"Social Programs: Reagan's Unkindest Cut," Editorial, *San Jose Mercury News*, 13 January 1983, n. pag.

III. Philosophical and Cultural Perspectives

THE MYTHS ABOUT POVERTY AND HUNGER IN AMERICA

Frances Moore Lappé

To most of us, the poverty trap refers to the plight of the poor. But the poverty trap has ensnared us all! It is a dependency on outworn and false beliefs that has trapped Western society for centuries.

For fifteen years, I have focused on the appropriate response of Americans to widespread and growing deprivation in the Third World. Turning my attention closer to home, in recent years I made a startling discovery: many of the same beliefs that color our view of the Third World determine how we perceive poverty in our own midst.

These beliefs are so pervasive as to be invisible. Our religion teaches us compassion—"Do unto others . . . Whatever you do to the least of these, you do to me." But in examining actual conditions, we find evidence of children physically stunted from lack of food, while virtually next door others appear overloaded with astounding surfeit. What beliefs could be so powerful as to override all of this culture's formal ethical teaching and the instinctive feelings of compassion that have evolved in the human heart?

I will suggest six myths. The first three concern the causes of poverty; the other three involve solutions—or the lack of them.

Myth No. 1: *Poverty and hunger result from natural forces beyond human control.*

Africa's current drought reinforces what most of us have always believed: human beings will forever be victims of nature.

We seldom stop to ponder a difficult question: why is it that although climate has not changed significantly, the number of deaths from natural disasters leapt sixfold between the 1960s and the 1970s?

This finding—by the Swedish Red Cross—suggests that although drought and flood are usually outside human control, their impact is not. Indeed, civilization might be defined as the construction of social institutions to protect us from just such ravages of nature. The present drought in Africa is not the cause but a trigger that reveals the breakdown of protective social structures.

The domestic version of this belief is more subtle. Here, we have created our own "natural laws." That is, we have placed certain rules of economic life above human control: to intervene, we are made to believe, is to court the wrath of God.

Foremost of these rules is the law of the market. The market distributes goods in the marketplace. It is fair because we all get to cast dollar-ballots. Some get more, others less, but what is the alternative? For intervening will destroy not only the market but our freedom as well.

Bowing before the market we accept also the inevitability of joblessness: industrial modernization necessarily means fewer jobs. And unemployment is the only way to control inflation. Isn't it?

From the Left comes another version: capitalism is incapable of generating full employment because capital must have a reserve— the jobless—in order to maintain profits.

But instead of viewing such laws as above our values, what would it mean to make the market serve our values? A first step is simply deciding what is appropriately distributed by the market and what is not. In my view, it is inappropriate to leave what is necessary to life itself to the vagaries of the market. Many others, even in capitalist economies, agree: every Western industrial country, except the United States, has, for example, removed health care from the market.

Second, we must simply recognize that much of what we have thought of as market-determined actually results from social choices for which we must take responsibility. The number of jobs, for example, is partly a function of how long each person works. Historically, pressures from trade unions and advances in technology have reduced work hours. If we want more jobs, why can we not continue this historical progression, which has been stymied for the past 40 years? Moreover, government decisions, including tax in-

centives, interest rates, and military versus civilian spending, determine the number of available jobs. Thus, the question is not whether the government intervenes, but what are its—our society's—
priorities? Of the $30 billion the government spends on employ-
ment, $28 billion goes for unemployment insurance that creates
neither new jobs nor useful goods or services. Why not use part of
these resources to create jobs and train workers? Moreover, that low
unemployment invariably leads to unacceptable inflation is hardly
an iron law. Between 1973 and 1980, Sweden's inflation rate (ten
percent was similar to ours (nine percent), but its unemployment
rate (1.9 percent) was less than one-third of ours (6.8 percent). This
suggests that many factors determine the rate of inflation, not
simply the number of people employed.

So the first self-defeating belief—applicable to our view of poverty here in America just as to poverty in the Third World—is that
we are at the mercy of immutable economic laws. We are not.

Myth No. 2: *Hunger and poverty result from scarcity.*

With people starving on television right before our eyes, it is
easy to forget that the world produces enough for every man,
woman, and child to consume 3,000 calories daily in just grain
alone. Even Africa could feed itself, according to a recent United
Nations study. Most of the best land in the hungriest countries
grows food for export.

Since it would seem silly to blame hunger in America on a
scarcity of food—when price-depressing overproduction is the
bane of farmers and 40 percent of our cropland produces for
export—our version of the scarcity myth is a belief in the scarcity of
jobs or of government resources to aid the poor.

In a society as rich as ours, do we really need to be reminded
that we do have the resources to feed, clothe, and house everyone at
a decent standard of living? Berkeley economist Benjamin Ward
estimates that this could be accomplished with half the current
output of the United States economy.

Many correctly challenge this notion of scarcity by arguing that
current antipoverty expenditures account for less than 10 percent
of the federal budget. Others—also correctly—argue that social
spending is not a drag on growth. Many European countries whose
economies outperformed ours during much of the past 20 years
devoted a much greater share of their GNP to social spending.

The unfortunate implication of these arguments, however, is that ending poverty may be a burden, just not too great a burden. Instead we must challenge Americans to see that the real burden is not a line-item in the federal budget. The real burden is not welfare spending. The real burden *is* poverty itself.

Poverty deprives all of us, not just the poor. The immediate costs include greater violence, crime, and disease, and downward pressure on all our wages. But most important is the untold loss of our collective potential, if we define poverty as the systematic denial of opportunity to fulfill one's innate potential, every poverty statistic hides millions of doctors, musicians, waiters, journalists, construction workers, artists, engineers, bus drivers, and athletes whose energies and talents were robbed from us by poverty. Only if we learn to see this invisible cost, will we begin to appreciate the real burden on all of us—not of ending poverty, but of poverty itself.

Myth No. 3: *Hunger and poverty result from innate human frailties.*

If Third World peasants just were not so culture-bound, if they were willing to modernize production, then hunger might be eliminated. This is the myth. It ignores the fact that in the Third World, the small producer, not the big, invariably produces the most per acre.

In America a parallel belief that poverty is caused by innate human proclivities takes many shapes. In its nastiest form, it emerges as racial bias. In 1981, 43 percent of whites queried said that laziness was a major cause of black unemployment. In a more sophisticated form, the belief is that no one will work if there is another way to survive. And the problem is that well-intended but dangerously mistaken do-gooders set up social programs that remove the necessity of work.

The crux of this argument, popularized recently in Charles Murray's book, *Losing Ground*, is simple: welfare allows people to choose not to work and therefore, in effect, to choose poverty. Thus, the more social welfare spending, the more poor people. But a careful look at the data contradicts Murray's simple equation. From 1950 to 1969, poverty decreased rapidly while public assistance spending more than doubled in real terms. From 1969 to 1977, the poverty rate varied while public assistance spending rose about 80 percent. Then, in the most recent period, poverty increased dramatically while government spending declined.

Obviously, poverty is not caused by welfare. The rate of poverty has increased—but not because of generous welfare spending. Between 1978 and 1983, some 9 million Americans sunk from the middle class into poverty—not just because they chose welfare, but because a shrinking number of jobs in America pay middle-class wages, because joblessness increased and because social spending was cut. And on top of these assaults, the poor were made to pay a larger share of their income in taxes after 1981.

Neither does the widespread view of the poor as a trapped underclass fit the facts. Sure, some have given up, but they are trapped by hopelessness, not by welfare. Moreover, the majority of poor are struggling to get out of poverty: the average length of time on welfare is about two years. About 50 percent of those below the poverty line are in the labor force, and among the minority of poor receiving welfare, almost one half have earned incomes. The problem is that work is not necessarily an escape from poverty.

Another way Americans often blame the poor for their poverty is to assume that they lack the proper "work ethic." Yet a 1970s study by the Brookings Institution found no significant differences in work attitudes between those receiving welfare and other Americans.

Similarly the argument that people "choose" poverty by failing to acquire requisite skills may seem reasonable until we look at the evidence. Economist David Gordon's revealing book *The Working Poor* concludes: "In at least two-thirds of all occupations in the economy, workers' employment success—measured by their wages or annual incomes—bears almost no relationship to their formal 'skills' training and is almost completely determined by the characteristics of the industries and jobs in which they work." A worker entering the automobile industry, for example, may have the same skills as one starting in the tobacco industry. The difference in the trajectory of their work lives—one up into the middle class and the other trapped in poverty—comes about because the interests of the auto worker are protected by a union. Today, unionized workers receive wages one-third higher than those of non-union workers.

In sum, Americans do not become poor by making the wrong choices. They are poor because they have no options. Welfare is no escape. Work at a minimum-wage job is no escape. Wages in trade and services, where most new jobs are and where 80 percent of employed women work, are notoriously low. (No wonder two-thirds of poor adults are women. According to the Department of Labor, half of production workers in 1981 earned hourly wages so low that, even if they managed to avoid unemployment for the entire year, their income still fell below the poverty line for a family of four. And our economy is not generating skilled work. In the next ten years, there will be fifteen times as many jobs for janitors as for computer technicians!

Myth No. 4: *All of us cannot make it, so our motto must be "sink or swim." The strong will survive.*

The international version of this belief, popularized by Dr. Garrett Hardin, is the most blood-chilling of the hunger myths—"lifeboat ethics." The weakest must be left to drown for the sake of the survival of those who remain. The Institute for Food and Development Policy has refuted this myth not only by documenting the untapped agricultural potential of countries such theories would push overboard, but by demonstrating that the heaviest burdens on world resources come from the industrialized countries so eager to blame "burdensome" Third World. The industrial countries are the world's biggest importers of agricultural commodities.

The domestic version of this myth tells us to be "realistic." Greater attempts to help the poor will drag down the rest of the economy. We have learned from experience. After all, spending on the Great Society programs of the 1960s helped generate our current economic problems.

Both the international and domestic versions of the lifeboat myth originate in the widespread misunderstanding that today's suffering results from actual scarcity: we see the "hungry hordes" of the Third World, or the downtrodden unemployed of our own inner cities, as an obstacle rather than a potential source of wealth.

We believe that tolerating unemployment saves us the burden of putting people to work. Instead, it robs us of the wealth their employment would create. Economists Sam Bowles and David Gordon estimate that the recession of the early 1980s, with its high levels of unemployment and idle factories, cost the economy almost $1 trillion in lost output. Political scientist Michael Harrington estimates that in 1982 the effects of increased unemployment and idle factories accounted for half of the huge federal deficit.

But for the many Americans who find the lifeboat solution distasteful there is another, more common belief about alleviating hunger.

Myth No. 5: *Charity is the answer to poverty, or if not the answer, at least it alleviates suffering.*

Many well-meaning Americans devote their energies to increasing and improving our foreign aid, blind to its real function. The Reagan administration has now stated what before was implicit: the goal of United States foreign aid is to shore up our strategic and military allies. This year, on a per capita basis, Central American allies will receive much more food aid than famine-stricken Africa.

Here at home, a similar kind of thinking also blinds us. Since we assume that only the poor suffer from poverty, the answer is for the well-off to give more. Charity-thinking blinds us to the many ways the increasing division between rich and poor undermines the quality of all our lives. Do we want to become like the Third World, divided between those few who live by their wealth and those many unable to live by their work? If we accept as inevitable the growing gap between rich and poor, we forsake the very character that our nation's founders saw as essential to democracy—a relative equality of condition. Thomas Jefferson, for example, strongly believed that constant vigilance against economic concentration was the only hope for democracy.

Myth No. 6: *There is a trade-off between fairness and efficiency. Fairness just does not work.*

On the basis of this belief, I hear people defend concentration of land ownership in the Third World, where typically less than 10 percent of the landowners control more than three-quarters of the land. Land reform, they argue, would result in lower production because the big growers have the size and know-how to make the land produce. Domestically, we accept that we must reward the rich and give even freer reign to giant corporations if we expect the economy to produce.

But produce *what* for *whom?* This is the critical question. In the Third World, if the majority has access neither to land nor jobs, they cannot make a demand in the marketplace for the goods they need. Naturally, the big growers seek the highest paying market, shifting production to luxury exports. At home, as policies further undermine the poor and reward the rich, boutiques and luxury condos flourish while the basic food and housing needs of the poor go unmet.

Moreover, as the roots of this growing chasm between rich and poor are exposed in the unfairness of our society's basic rules—tax, credit, and wage policies that reward wealth over work, the entire fabric of our society begins to shred. Only the presumption of basic fairness can hold a non-authoritarian society together. In other words, we do not have the luxury of choosing efficiency over fairness—fairness is the only way that works.

These six myths are in essence one: poverty is inevitable and attempts to solve it directly only make it worse. These six beliefs reflect a profound sense of human powerlessness.

I am convinced that anthropologists of future centuries looking back on the primitive cultures that have inhabited the North American continent would find some bewildering contrasts. The original American Indian cultures, with no knowledge of the microbial world, believed that disease could not be passed from one person to another; disease was a sign from the gods. Hundreds of years later, the dominant North American civilization, having achieved amazing knowledge of the origin and control of disease, still clung to the belief that social distress—poverty and hunger— was beyond its capacity to eliminate.

If it is this sense of powerlessness that lies at the root of poverty and hunger, we must stop confusing people by implying that more of the same—increased welfare spending alone, for example—will end poverty. Instead we must work to understand *why* people feel powerless and what it takes to address that powerlessness.

We Americans, I believe, feel powerlessness before the complexity and size of our economic institutions. Thus we conclude that the economy must be run either by big business or by the immutable laws of the market. Second, while telecommunications has theoretically turned us into a "global village," our lack of real contact across class and race lines convinces us that we cannot generalize from our own experience (Those poor people just are not like us). Finally, we are so sure that our forebears created the best of all possible systems we are unable to look critically at its underlying rules.

Indeed, our sense of powerlessness is appropriate and will continue until we see that the principle of democracy—the accountability of decision-makers—is our most cherished inheritance, not a particular economic form. Betraying this heritage, we have allowed a corporate economy to emerge that is not accountable to those whose lives it touches. Our nation's founders rejected monarchy, but have we allowed the same notion to arise once more, only in a new form?

We can begin to build on the best of our heritage by rethinking "rights and responsibilities" essential to democracy. Is it logical to educate people to contribute to society and then not assure them the right to do so? Does not the promise of democracy require that we add to our democratic rights the right to employment at a living wage?

Our conception of democracy, however, must not stop at the corporate door. As long as Americans have no say in the organization of their work, as long as so many hate their work and live in fear of work-place hazards and joblessness, they will remain defensive, suspicious of those who appear not to be sacrificing as much as they are: *the poor*. Thus, initiatives to democratize the work-place—through stronger and more accountable unions and worker participation and ownership—cannot only ameliorate the poverty of working life but can contribute to altering the assumptions that divide us, assumptions that make poverty inevitable.

I am not suggesting a solution. I am offering a direction. We can regain a sense of power over the direction of our lives and our society only by examining our most deeply held values—including democracy itself. As citizens of the world's first political democracy, our birthright should include a belief in the possibility of what has before seemed impossible. To end poverty we must let go of many destructive myths blocking our path. We can move forward—not by scolding, not by pretending that half-way measures work—but by re-examining our most deeply held values in order to attain an economic life worthy of our democratic heritage.

RIGHTS, OBLIGATIONS AND WORLD HUNGER

Onora O'Neill

Hunger and Famine

Some of the facts of world hunger and poverty are now widely known. Among them are the following six:

1. World population is now over 5 billion and rising rapidly. It will exceed 6 billion by end of this century.
2. In many Third World countries investment and growth have so far concentrated in an urbanized modern sector, whose benefits reach a minority.
3. In many poor countries the number of destitute and landless increases even when there is economic growth.
4. In many African countries harvests have been falling for two decades and dependence on imported grain is growing.
5. The rich countries of the North (for these purposes "the North" means the countries of North America, the EEC, and Australasia!) grow vast surpluses of grain. The grain which goes to poor countries is mostly sold.
6. The rural poor of the Third World are sometimes harmed by grain imports, which are distributed in towns, so depriving peasants of customers for their crops. These peasants then migrate to shanty towns.

And then there is Ethiopia. We can understand the famine in Ethiopia better in the wider context of world hunger. Famines are not unexpected natural catastrophes, but simply the harshest ex-

treme of hunger. We know well enough where in the world poverty
and hunger are constantly bad enough for minor difficulties to
escalate into famine. Ethiopia had its last famine only ten years ago.
We know which other regions in Africa, Asia and Latin America are
now vulnerable to famines. Famine is the tip of the iceberg of
hunger. It is the bit that is publicized and to which we react; but the
greater part of the suffering is less lurid and better hidden.

Most hungry people are not migrating listlessly or waiting for
the arrival of relief supplies. They are leading their normal lives
with their normal economic, social and familial situations, earning
and growing what they normally earn or grow, yet are always poor
and often hungry. These normal conditions are less spectacular
than famine, but affect far more people.

We are tempted to set famine aside from other, endemic hunger
and poverty. We blame natural catastrophes such as floods,
drought, blight, or cold for destroying crops and producing famines. But harsh circumstances cause famines only when social and
economic structures are too fragile to absorb such natural shocks.
Californians know that desert climates need not lead to famines.
Minnesotans know that a ferocious winter need not be reflected in
countless annual deaths from cold. Yet both regions would have
catastrophic annual mortality if they lacked appropriate social and
economic structures. Many natural catastrophes produce human
catastrophes only when social structures are inadequate.

Focus on Action

We could list the facts of world hunger, poverty and famine
endlessly. But facts alone do not tell us what to do. What surely
matters is action. But here we meet a problem. Which action we
advocate depends partly on our perception of the facts, and this
perception itself depends partly on the particular ethical outlook
we adopt. Both our perception of problems and our prescriptions
for action reflect our ethical theory. Ethical theories are not elegant
trimmings which decorate our reasoning about practical problems.
They determine our entire focus. They lead us to see certain facts
and principles as salient and others as insubstantial. They focus our
action—or our inertia.

I shall here consider three theories of what ought to be done
about hunger and famine. Two are widely known and discussed in
present debates in the English speaking world, while the third,

though in many ways older and more familiar, now receives rather less public attention. I shall offer certain criticisms of the two prevailing approaches and recommend the third to your attention.

The first approach is one that makes human happiness and well being the standard for assessing action. Its most common modern version is *utilitarianism*. For utilitarians all ethical requirements are basically a matter of beneficence to others. The second approach takes respect for human rights as basic and interprets the central issues of world hunger as matters of justice, which can be secured if all rights are respected. The third approach takes fulfillment of human obligations as basic and insists that these obligations include both obligations of justice and obligations of help or beneficence to others, and above all to others in need. Since no famine policy or development strategy would be adequate if it guided only individual action, all three of these positions will be considered as ways in which public and institutional policies as well as individual action might be guided.

Measuring and Maximizing Happiness

The central idea of all ethical reasoning which focuses on consequences or results is that action is right if it produces good results. The specifically utilitarian version of such thinking insists that the goodness of results be assessed by their contribution to total human happiness, and specifically that the best results are those that maximize human happiness. This position is very familiar to many of us because restricted versions of it are incorporated in economic theory and in business practice, and often used in daily decision making. It leads naturally to the question: what will maximize human happiness?

This seems such a simple question, but it has been given many unclear answers. Even discussions of hunger and famine, where the means to greater happiness may seem obvious, jangle with incompatible claims. The debates of the last decade show radical disagreements between utilitarian writers on world hunger.

The Australian philosopher, Peter Singer, has used simple economic considerations to argue that any serious utilitarian should undertake radical redistribution of his or her possessions and income to the poor. Standard marginalist considerations suggest that we can increase happiness by transferring resources from the rich to the poor. Any unhappiness caused by the loss of a luxury—such as a car—will be more than outweighed by the happiness produced by using the same funds to buy essential food for the hungry.

But the United States writer on famine, population and ecological problems, Garrett Hardin, argues on the contrary that help to the poorest is forbidden on utilitarian grounds because it will in the end lead to the greatest misery. Drawing on the thought of the early nineteenth century economist and population theorist Thomas Malthus, he argues that food given to the poor will lead to population increases and ultimately to more people than can be fed and so ultimately to devastating famine and maximal misery.

It is an urgent practical question whether utilitarians can resolve these disagreements. The founder of utilitarianism, the late eighteenth century radical philosopher and polemicist, Jeremy Bentham, thought we could do so with scientific rigor: it was only a matter of measuring and aggregating seven dimensions of human happiness. To help us he provided a pithy mnemonic verse in his *Introduction to the Principles of Morals and of Legislation*:

> *Intense, long, certain, speedy, fruitful, pure,*—Such marks in *pleasures* and in *pains* endure. Such pleasures seek if *private* be thy end: If it be *public* wide let them *extend*[1].

But this is simply not enough. Despite the recurrent optimism of some economists and decision theorists about measuring happiness in limited contexts, we know we cannot generally predict or measure or aggregate happiness with any precision.

Accuracy, Precision and Needs

Yet we can, it seems, often make approximate judgments of human happiness. And perhaps that is enough. After all, we do not need great precision, but only reasonable (even if vague) accuracy. We know that hunger and destitution mean misery and that enough to eat ends that sort of misery. Do we need to know more?

If we are to be utilitarians we do need to know more. We need not only to know what general result to aim at, but to work out what means to take. Since very small changes in actions and policies may vastly alter results, precise comparisons of many results are indispensable. Examples of some unsuspected results of intended beneficence make the point vivid. Some food aid policies have actually harmed those whom they were intended to benefit or to benefit those who were not in the first place the poorest. (This is not to say that food aid is dispensable—especially in cases of famine—but it is never enough to end misery, and it can be damaging if misdirected.) Some aid policies aimed at raising standards of life, for example by encouraging farmers to grow cash crops, have damaged the livelihood of subsistence farmers, and harmed the poorest. The benefits of aid are often diverted to those who are not in the greatest need. The ubiquity of corruption also shows how essential it is for utilitarians to make precise and not vague judgments about how to increase human happiness. Benevolent intentions are quite easy to identify; but beneficent policies cannot be identified if we cannot predict and compare results precisely.

To do their calculations utilitarians need not only precise measurements of happiness, but precise prediction of which policies lead to which results. They need the sort of comprehensive and predictive social science to which many researchers have aspired, but not attained. At present we cannot resolve even very basic disagreements between rival utilitarians. We cannot show whether happiness is maximized by attending to nearby desires where we can intervene personally (even if these are desires that reflect no needs), or by concentrating all our help on the neediest. Indeed, we often know too little even to predict which public policies will benefit the poor most.

If utilitarians somehow developed the precise methods of prediction and calculation that they lack, the results might not endorse help for the poor. Utilitarian thinking assigns no special importance to human need. Happiness produced by meeting the desires of those around us—even their desires for unneeded goods—may count as much as, or more than, happiness produced by ending real misery. All that matters is which desire is more intense. Since the neediest may be so weakened and apathetic that they no longer have strong desires, their need may count less and not more in a utilitarian calculus. But we know that charity that begins at home, where others' desires are evident to us, can find so much to do there that it often ends at home too. So we can see that unless needs are given a certain priority in ethical thinking they may be greatly neglected.

Meanwhile utilitarian thinking unavoidably leaves vital dilemmas unclarified and unresolved. Was it beneficent, and so right, to negotiate massive development loans, although soaring interest rates have meant that much of poor countries' export earnings are now swallowed by interest payments? The present rich countries developed during a period of low and stable interest rates: they now control the ground rules of a world economy which does not provide that context of opportunity for remaining poor countries. Has it been happiness maximizing to provide development loans for poor countries in these conditions? Might happiness not be greater if poor countries had relied on lesser but indigenous sources of investment? Or would the cost of slower growth have been a larger total of human misery which could have been avoided by higher interest rates?

These are bitter questions and I do not know the answer in general or for particular countries. I raise them as an example of the difficulty of relying on predictions and calculations about maximal happiness in determining what ought to be done, and what it would be wrong to do.

The Human Rights Movement

The difficulties of utilitarian thinking may seem to arise from its ambitious scope. Utilitarianism tries to encompass the whole of morality under a single principle, and to select acts and policies which are not only right, but best or optimal. One alternative might be to aim for rather less. This might be done by looking at principles for evaluating acts and rejecting those that are wrong, rather than at grand proposals to find just those acts and policies which provide optimal results.

The most common contemporary embodiment of this approach is that of the human rights movement, which I shall consider next. The rhetoric of human rights is all around us—perhaps never more so than at present in the English speaking world, and particularly in the United States. The sources of the rhetoric are well known. The earlier ones are the grand eighteenth century documents, such as Tom Paine's *The Rights of Man*, and the declaration of rights of the United States and the French revolutions. The more recent growth of concern for human rights reflects a considerable revival of such thinking in the post World War II search for foundations for a new international order, which gave rise to various United Nations documents, such as the Universal Declaration of Human Rights of 1948. The modern human rights movement gained impetus from the commitment of the Carter administration to a foreign policy which hoped to secure respect for human rights in other countries. While the Reagan administration and the Thatcher government have not taken a comprehensive commitment to human rights to heart, both have based their political outlook on a certain restricted picture of human rights, in which rights to property and one range of economic freedoms are given special emphasis. All these approaches take the central ethical requirement in human affairs to be respect for justice and construe justice as a matter of respect for rights.

Liberty Rights and Welfare Rights

Within the tradition of discussion of human rights there is considerable disagreement about the list of rights which justice comprises. In general terms, the more right wing proponents of the tradition assert that there are only rights to liberty, hence that we have only the corresponding obligations of non-interference with others' liberty. Other more left wing proponents of human rights assert that there are also certain "welfare" rights, hence certain positive obligations to help and assist others. Those who think that all rights are liberty rights point to supposed rights to life, liberty and the pursuit of happiness, including the right to unregulated economic activity. On this view it is unjust to interfere with others' exercise of democratic political rights or capitalist economic rights. Those who think that there are also "welfare" rights point to supposed rights to food or basic health care or welfare payments. Since rights to unregulated economic activity are incompatible with these, they reject unrestricted economic "rights."

These disagreements cannot be settled by appeal to documents. The United Nations documents were a political compromise and resolutely confer *all* sorts of rights. Proponents of liberty rights therefore think that these documents advocate some spurious "rights," which are neither part of nor compatible with justice. However, it is worth remembering that this political compromise has in fact been accepted by nearly all governments, who therefore have a prima facie institutionalized treaty obligation to enact both liberty and "welfare" rights. This can be an awkward point given that many people in the West tend to fault the Eastern block countries for their violation of liberty rights but to overlook the systematic denial in the West of certain economic and welfare rights (such as a right to employment) which the international documents endorse.

Human Rights and Human Needs

It matters hugely for the destitute which interpretation of rights is acceptable and is used to guide policies and decisions. If human rights are all liberty rights, then justice to the poor and hungry is achieved by *laissez faire*—provided we do not curtail their liberties all is just. For example, if a transnational suddenly closes its operations in a poor country, so devastating the local economy, no injustice has been done. Or if the IMF requires severe economic retrenchment so that interest payments can be made, this is just, whatever hardships are inflicted. Or if commodity price shifts leave those who depend on a single cash crop—such as coffee, rubber or palm oil—greatly impoverished, this is just, since no liberties will have been violated. If all human rights are liberty rights, then the needs of the poor are of no concern in working out what may be done without injustice.

But if some human rights are welfare or economic rights, justice will require that some of these needs be met. For example, if there are rights to food or to subsistence then it is unjust not to meet these needs, and unjust not to regulate any economic activities which will prevent their being met. However, any claim that there are "welfare" rights is mere rhetoric unless the corresponding obligations are justified and allocated. And here the advocates of human rights are often evasive. It is a significant and not a trivial matter that there is no human obligations movement.

Rights, Liberty and Autonomy

These disputes cannot be settled unless we can show which rights there are. The eighteenth century pioneers often claimed that certain rights were self-evident. This claim now seems brazen, and in any case cannot settle disputes between the advocates of different sets of rights. The most impressive line of argument aimed at settling these disputes takes it that human rights constitute collectively the largest possible realization of human *liberty* or of human *autonomy*. However, even if we could justify assuming that either liberty or autonomy is the most fundamental of moral concerns, these two approaches lead to quite divergent claims about what rights there are. In addition, the advocates of each approach often disagree among themselves about exactly which rights there are.

Those who think that what is fundamental is *liberty*, understood as mere, "negative" non-interference by others, allow only for liberty rights. The idea of a consistent partitioning of human liberty would collapse as soon as we try to add rights to receive help or services, for the obligations which make these "welfare" rights a reality will be incompatible with various rights of action which basic liberty rights include. If we are obligated to provide food for all who need it, we cannot have unrestricted rights to do what we want with any food we have. At best certain societies may use their liberty rights to set up institutionalized rights to certain benefits—e.g. to education, welfare, health care—as has been done in most of the economically advanced nations. But an institutionalized right is not a natural or human right. The rights institutionalized in the developed countries have no bearing on the hunger and poverty in the Third World, where such rights have not been set up.

Those who think that it is autonomy rather than mere noninterference that is fundamental insist that there are some "welfare" rights to goods and services, such as a right to subsistence. For without adequate nutrition and shelter, human autonomy is destroyed, and liberty rights themselves would be pointless. But the advocates of subsistence rights have so far produced no convincing arguments to show who should bear obligations to feed others. Yet this is the question that matters most if "rights to subsistence" are to meet human needs.

Rights and Charity

Many advocates of human rights point out that we should not worry too much if rights theory neglects human needs. We should remember that justice is not the whole of morality, which can also require voluntarily given help. The needs of the poor can be met by charity. This thought appeals to many people. But it is an unconvincing one in the context of a theory of human rights. The rights perspective itself undercuts the status of charity, regarding it not as any sort of obligation, but as something that we are free to do or to omit, a matter of supererogation rather than of obligation. Such a view of help for the needy may be comfortable for the "haves" of this world, since it suggests that they go beyond duty and do something especially good if they help others at all. But it is depressing for the "have-nots" who cannot claim help of anybody, since it is not a matter of right. They can just hope help will happen; and usually what happens will be witheringly inadequate.

Human Agency, Rights and Obligations

Justice need not be understood in the terms either of the human rights movement or of the utilitarian view of justice as just one contribution among others to human happiness. One way in which a different approach can be taken is by looking first at obligations rather than at rights. This has been a standard approach to ethical questions, both before and throughout the Christian tradition. Rights are eighteenth century upstarts in moral discourse, as is the elevation of individual happiness to be the arbiter of moral judgment. Both these approaches see human beings in a somewhat passive way. This is plain enough in the utilitarian picture of human beings as loci of pains and pleasures. But it is less obvious that men and women are seen as passive in the theory of human rights. On the contrary, the turn to rights is sometimes defended on the grounds that it assigns a more active role to the powerless, who are to see themselves as wronged claimants rather than as the humble petitioners of more traditional, feudal pictures.

It is true that the human rights movement sees human beings *more* as agents than did feudal and theories. But it still does not see them as fully autonomous: claimants basically agitate for others to act. When we claim liberty rights or rights of authority our first demand is that others act, so yielding us a space or opportunity in which we may or may not act. When we claim "welfare" rights we need not picture ourselves as acting at all, but must see whoever bears the corresponding obligations as acting. By contrast, when we talk about obligations we are speaking directly to those agents and agencies with the power to produce or refuse changes—the very audience which the rights perspective addresses only indirectly.

The French philosopher Simone Weil, writing during the Second World War, put the point this way in *The Need for Roots*:

> The notion of obligations comes before that of rights, which is subordinate and relative to the former. A right is not effectual by itself, but only in relation to the obligation to which it corresponds, the effective exercise of a right springing not from the individual who possesses it, but from other men who consider themselves as being under a certain obligation towards him.[2]

We do not know what a right amounts to until we know who has what obligation to do what for whom under which circumstances. When we try to be definite about rights we always have to talk about obligations.

A fundamental difficulty with the rhetoric of rights is that it addresses only part—and the less powerful part—of the relevant audience. This rhetoric may have results if the poor are not wholly powerless; but where they are, claiming rights provides meager pickings. When the poor are powerless it is the powerful who must be convinced that they have certain obligations—whether or not the beneficiaries claim the performance of these obligations as their right. The first concern of an ethical theory which focuses on action should be obligations, rather than rights.

What Obligations of Justice Are There?

A theory of obligations can help deliberation about world hunger only if it is possible to show what obligations human beings have. The effort to show this without reliance on theological assumptions was made in the eighteenth century by the German philosopher Immanuel Kant. Recently Kant's work has often been seen as one more theory of human rights. This may be because he based his argument for human obligations on a construction analogous to that used in thinking of human rights as a partitioning of maximal human liberty or autonomy. For he asks what principles of action could consistently be shared by all agents. The root idea behind such a system of principles is that human obligations are obligations never to act in ways in which others cannot in principle also act. The fundamental principles of action must be shareable, rather than principles available only to a privileged few. Kant's method of determining the principles of obligation cannot be applied to the superficial detail of action: we evidently cannot eat the very grain another eats or have every one share the same roof. But we can try to see that the deep principles of our lives and of our institutions are shareable by all, and then work out the implications of these deep principles for particular situations.

If we use the Kantian construction we can reach some interesting conclusions about human obligations. One obligation of justice that emerges from the construction is that of non-coercion. For a fundamental principle of coercion in some matter cannot be shared by all, since those who are coerced are prevented from acting, and so cannot share the principle of action. Coercion, we might say with Kant, is not *universalizable*.

This argument alone does not tell us what non-coercion requires in particular situations. Clearly it rules out many things that respect for liberty rights rules out. For example, a principle of non-coercion rules out killing, maiming, assaulting, and threatening others. This range of obligations not to coerce are as important for the well-fed as for the hungry. But other aspects of non-coercion are peculiarly important for the hungry. Those who aim to act on a principle of non-coercion must take account of the fact that it is always rather easy to coerce those who are weak or vulnerable by activities that would not coerce richer or more powerful people.

Avoiding coercion is not just a matter of avoiding a short list of interferences in others' action, as rights approaches would have us imagine. Avoiding coercion means making sure that in our dealings with others we leave them room either to accept or to refuse the offers and suggestions made. This shows why an emphasis on obligations not to coerce is particularly telling in evaluating our dealings with the poor: they are so easily coerced. We can make them "offers they cannot refuse" with the greatest of ease. What might be genuine offers among equals, which others can accept or reject, can be threatening and unrefusable for the needy and vulnerable. They can be harmed in ways that threaten life by standard commercial or legal procedures, such as business deals which locate dangerous industrial processes in urban areas, or exact stiff political concessions for investment, or for what passes as aid, or which set harsh commercial conditions on "aid," such as mandating unneeded imports from a "donor" nation.

Arrangements of these sorts can coerce even when they use the outward forms of commercial bargaining and legality. These forms of bargaining are designed for use between agents of roughly equal power. They may not be enough to protect the powerless. Hence both individuals and agencies such as corporations and national governments (both of the North and of the South) and aid agencies must meet exacting standards if they are not to coerce the vulnerable in ordinary legal, diplomatic and commercial dealings. Economic or material justice cannot be achieved without avoiding institutionalized as well as individual forms of coercion.

A second fundamental obligation of justice is that of avoiding deception. A principle of deception, too, is not universalizable, because victims of deception, like victims of coercion, are in principle precluded from sharing the perpetrator's principle of action, which is kept hidden from them. However, since the obligation of non-deception is relevant to all public and political life, and not solely for dealings which affect the poor, the hungry and the vulnerable (although they are more easily deceived), I shall not explore its implications here.

Obligations to Help: Emergency Relief, Development and Respect

In a rights framework the whole of our moral obligations are brought under the heading of justice. But an obligations approach of the Kantian type also justifies obligations which are not obligations of justice and whose performance cannot be claimed as rights. Some types of action cannot be done for all others, so they cannot be a universal obligation or have corresponding rights. Yet they also are not contingent on any special relationship, so they cannot be a matter of special, institutionalized obligation. Yet they can be a matter of obligation. A theory of obligation, unlike a theory of rights, can allow for "imperfect" obligations, which are not allocated to specified recipients and so cannot be claimed.

This provides a further way in which an appreciation of need can enter into a theory of human obligations. We know that others in need are vulnerable and not self-sufficient. It follows that, even if they are not coerced, they may be unable to act, and so unable to become or remain autonomous agents who could act on principles which can be universally shared. Hence, if our fundamental commitment is to treat others as agents who could share the same principles that we act on, then we must be committed equally to strategies and policies that enable them to become and to remain agents. If we do anything less, we do not view others as doers like ourselves. However, nobody and no agent can do everything to sustain the autonomy of all others. Hence obligations to help are not and cannot be obligations to meet all needs; but they can be obligations not to base our lives on principles that are indifferent to or neglectful of others' need and what it actually takes to sustain their agency. In particular situations such "imperfect" obligations may require specific and arduous action. The fact that we cannot help everyone only shows that we have no obligation to help everyone, and not that we have no obligation to help anyone.

If we are not indifferent or neglectful of the requirements for sustaining others' autonomy we will, I suggest, find ourselves committed not only to justice but to various further principles in our action towards the poor and vulnerable. First we will be committed to material help that sustains agency, by helping people over the threshold of poverty below which possibilities for autonomous action are absent or meager. Since sustained and systematic help is needed if vulnerability and dependence are not to recur endlessly, this implies a commitment to development policies as well as to emergency food aid.

Unreliable aid does not secure autonomy. But nor, of course, can withholding food aid in emergencies secure autonomy. Since human needs are recurrent, food aid is not enough. Food is eaten and is gone; help can secure others' agency only if it constructs social and economic institutions which can meet human needs on a sustained basis. This means that help to the poorest and most vulnerable must seek sustainable production to make sure that when a given cycle of consumption is past, more is in the pipeline. Development of the relevant sort is evidently not only an economic matter, it also includes the development of human skills by appropriate education and institutional changes which help poor and vulnerable people to gain some control over their lives.

Since the basis of these obligations to help is the claim that principles of action must be shareable by all, the pursuit of development must not itself reduce or damage others' agency. It must not fail to respect those who are helped. Their desires and views must be sought, and their participation respected. Agency is not fostered if the poor experience "donor" agencies as new oppressors. Others' autonomy is not sustained if they are left feeling that they have been the victims of good works.

Conclusions and Afterthoughts

The theory of obligations just sketched is surprisingly familiar to most of us. It is not distant from pictures of human obligation that we find in the Christian tradition, and in the idiom of much of our social life. And it chimes closely with other traditions too. Many of the voluntary aid agencies are fond of quoting a Chinese proverb which runs: give a man a fish and you feed him for a day; teach him to fish and you feed him for life. President Reagan too has quoted this saying.

Although the position is traditional and familiar, the favored ethical theories of today do not endorse it. Utilitarian perspectives endorse the pursuit of happiness without specific concern to meet needs; human rights perspectives do not vindicate obligations to help those in need. It therefore seems appropriate to end with some polemical questions rather than a feeling of reassurance. How and why have we allowed uncertain images of maximal happiness and self-centered visions of claiming human rights to distort

our understanding of central ethical notions such as justice, beneficence and respect for human agents? Why have so many people
been sure that our obligations to others are a matter of not interfer-
ing in their concerns—of doing . . . nothing?

If human obligations are based on the requirements for re-
specting and securing one another's agency, then we may find another of Simone Weil's remarks to the point:

> The obligation is only performed if the respect is effectively ex-
> pressed in a real, not a fictitious, way; and this can only be done
> through the medium of Man's earthly needs. . . . On this point, the
> human conscience has never varied. Thousands of years ago, the
> Egyptians believed that no soul could justify itself after death unless
> it could say, "I have never let anyone suffer from hunger." All
> Christians know they are liable to hear Christ say to them one day, "I
> was an hungered, and ye gave me no meat." Every one looks on
> progress as being, in the first place, a transition to a state of human
> society in which people will not suffer from hunger.[3]

To make that transition is indeed no longer a matter of feeding
the beggar at the gate. Modern opportunities are broader and
demand political as well as—perhaps more than—merely individual action. Of course, no individual can do everything. But this will
daunt only those who are riveted by an exclusively individual conception of human endeavor and success. If we remember that many
human activities and successes are not individual we need not be
daunted. We can then act in the knowledge that no individual and
no institution is prevented from making those decisions within its
power in ways which help fulfill rather than spurn obligations to
the hungry.

Notes

[1]Jeremy Bentham, *Introduction to the Principles of Morals and of Legislation* (New
York: Hafner Publishing Co., 1948), p. 29.

[2]Simone Weil, *The Need for Roots* (New York: Harper and Row, Publishers, 1952),
p. 3.

[3]Ibid., p.6.

IS POVERTY AN INJUSTICE?

Paul Steidl-Meier

Introduction: The Specter of Poverty

The specter of poverty has always been part of the human condition. At the same time people have never been able to remain indifferent to it. It is instructive to begin by recalling various attempts to account for poverty that have evolved in different cultures throughout history.

The existence of poverty has variously been attributed to fate and the inscrutable cosmic order of the universe, to the cruelty of an unjust God, to the sins of the poor, to laziness, and to class oppression. Prescriptions for dealing with it range from Stoic resignation, to identification with the cross of Christ, to revolution.

It is noteworthy that the major body of historical opinion on poverty does not view it as an injustice. There are exceptions of course; some forms of modern thought see it as an injustice of a cruel God and others as an injustice perpetrated by class oppression. But by far the dominant attitude has been that poverty was an inescapable fact of life and somehow deserved by those who suffered it. Christian tradition itself is paradoxical. Indigence itself is seen as a sin. In the face of it there has always been a sense of duty to give alms to those in need, to practice the corporal works of mercy, and in the spirit of the beatitudes, to give oneself in the service of others. The legitimacy of what the tradition called superfluous wealth was severely limited in the face of unmet needs of others.[1] In addition, there has always been an evangelical ideal of poverty in the faith community to which people such as Francis of Assisi provide an inspiring witness. But such evangelical poverty should not be confused with indigence. Rather it means, first of all, that all that we have, we have received as a gift from God; and, secondly, all that we have received we have received for the building up of the fellowship by sharing our gifts with others and serving them.[2] It would be a perversion of our gifts to merely convert them to personal riches. Evangelical poverty proposes a voluntary emptying of self, and a relinquishing of possessions, and the denial of the impulse to always have more for ourselves so that our neighbor might have more. But it does not mean indigence.

Yet Christian teaching on indigent poverty has not for the most part been characterized by a clarion call for social justice. The poor were usually spoken of as the objects of the charity of the rich. Part of the reason for this is found historically in an almost exclusive concentration upon a future eschatology where, as in the case of Dives and Lazarus, justice would be done in the final judgment of God. Another theological reason was found in a certain theology of the cross which urged the innocent to identify themselves with the innocent suffering of Christ; such suffering, it was argued, would purify the soul and would be salvific both for the one suffering as well as for others. Human suffering became redemptive as it was subsumed into the suffering and death of the Son of God himself.

When all is said and done, some popular versions of Christian theology maintained a paradoxical position of 1) providing the indigent with a rationale for resigning themselves to their condition, 2) urging those who had more to give alms out of their surplus and practice the works of mercy, 3) warning those who continued to amass superfluous wealth while others were needy that they were responsible for the suffering of the poor; that in their greed and pursuit of the folly of riches they were guilty of injustice and defacing the image of God. For all of this they would have to pay on the last day. All in all there was little call for structural change. This sociological point is of fundamental importance. Marx would characterize it as ideological collusion with the oppressive classes by providing opium to the people.

The real turning point in social attitudes towards indigent poverty came with the modern period and the enlightenment. The historians still use the words "modern" and "enlightenment" which reveals perhaps the magnitude of the cultural change that took place. With their emphasis upon reason and science and its dedication to a refashioned ideology of progress, the modernists provided a major catalyst to the rethinking of poverty.[3]

Progress could overcome poverty. The contributions of science

in the fields of medicine, agriculture, education, population control, as well as the industrial revolution held out the promise of
vanquishing poverty. But the promise was in part illusory as
Charles Dickens, Karl Marx, Henry George and others were to
point out. The new wealth which scientific capitalism generated
was not spread around but concentrated in the hands of a few. In
the image of Shakespeare's *Coriolanus* the belly was storing up food
and not sending it through the body.[4] A new vision of poverty rose
up which was grounded in the realities of exploitation. This viewpoint is still very much with us today: the system causes poverty.
But that was not the only modern vision nor has it been the dominant vision in North America where poverty has most frequently
been attributed to laziness. Against the backdrop of the Statue of
Liberty and the frontier, America was seen as a land of opportunity
from sea to shining sea.[5] To remain indigent in the midst of such
potential for wealth could only be traced to a lack of industry and
thrift. Both modern views see poverty as unnecessary. But one
position sees indigent poverty as a systemic injustice and the other
sees it as something which the poor fundamentally bring upon
themselves.

In the sixties a new consciousness of poverty was born in the
United States, stimulated to a great extent by Michael Harrington's
publication of *The Other America*.[6] The last twenty-five years have
witnessed great efforts to overcome poverty. We know more today
of both domestic and international poverty than ever before. Yet,
while the phenomenon of poverty is apparent, its nature remains
puzzling and programs to overcome it are invariably stymied. In
what follows I first discuss the meaning of poverty and then the
notion of justice. Then I make some applications both to the causes
of poverty as well as to the solutions. I conclude with some remarks
about the shaping of public policy in a pluralistic society.

The Meaning of Poverty

One of the problems with defining and measuring poverty is
that it is not a univocal notion. There are both different types of
poverty and various configurations of each type. What is the opposite of poverty? It is not wealth, although this is involved. It is
power. On the individual level, this lack of power is seen in the
deprivation of capacities and in fatalistic attitudes of hopelessness
and despair. On the social level it is in being subjects to the (political, economic or cultural) system rather than subjects of it.

Social scientists do not agree on the definition of poverty and its social indicators or upon its causes and solutions. The fundamental meaning of poverty is expressed in the absolute deprivation of human capacities.[7]

This means that on an individual level, a person's ability to do various things such as work, think, play, create or attain his or her goals is severely impaired. On a social level, poverty is a much more complex syndrome. It combines underconsumption, malnutrition, bad housing conditions, low educational levels and poor sanitary conditions with unstable or primitive participation in mechanisms of social integration and adherence to values different from those held by the rest of society.[8]

I find that Sen's position is closely related in outlook to the work of Abraham Maslow, who long ago articulated a view of human development in terms of being-needs and deficience-needs.[9] The focus of overall human development is the full self-actualization of the person. The poverty syndrome in an absolute sense is defined as the negation of such a prospect in terms of the deprivation of a person's capacities and manifests itself in severely limited access to commodities and resources, in physical weakness, vulnerability to contingencies, political, economic and cultural powerlessness, and isolation.

It is important to mention that in this context of absolute poverty one may speak of an opportunity cost approach to poverty. This measure estimates the social cost to society that permanent poverty represents in terms of lost productivity, the lack of market development, and so forth, which would have resulted had the undeveloped potential of the poor been developed. The notion is intuitively clear but remains very difficult to measure in precise terms. Usually the presentation is rhetorical and focuses upon the social benefits and costs that would have been lost had not Newton, Edison, Lincoln or other leading figures developed healthily. Obviously the tables could be turned in terms of the social costs of a figure like Hitler, Pol Pot or Idi Amin. Nonetheless, the opportunity cost notion remains useful for it underlines how poverty itself breeds more poverty.

Contrary to the above, many social scientists insist that poverty can only be defined relatively. They tend to take a more narrowly defined economic approach. There are three relative definitions of poverty. The first of these focuses upon baskets of commodities, incomes and resources needed to meet basic needs. However, neither the necessities of life nor the means to meet them are fixed. They are dynamic. They grow and develop and are constantly being reshaped. They are largely environmentally determined and can only be relatively established from place to place. A second approach to relative poverty highlights the inequalities in income distribution in a given society. The focus falls upon the comparative differences in living standards between, for example, the top 20% and the bottom 20%. A third relative approach is more arbitrary and tries to settle upon a poverty line which serves as a benchmark for public policy interventions. Poverty lines are not easy to construct. If the goal of such a policy is to capture a household's relative socioeconomic opportunity set, it is not clear that simply defining the target group as that population below "x" amount of income would be satisfactory.

Discussion of policy and social ethics becomes confused when it is unclear just what type of poverty one is talking about. My main concern is absolute poverty. Absolute poverty focuses upon a qualitative norm: the full development of the person's potential, both individually and socially. Basic human needs are defined in terms of the proper functioning of human capacities and the social minimum necessary to maintain health, the ability to work and be creative, and to live with dignity. The objective of policy to overcome poverty is, therefore, primarily qualitative. But, in a secondary way, much of what poverty is about can be relatively expressed in terms of this or that basket of commodities, income distribution ratios or benchmark income levels.

There are clearly many problems associated with the measurement of poverty. These are manifested both in the selection of criteria as well as in the research methodology which underlies empirical surveys. Suffice it to note that, given the definition of poverty based on human capacities, roughly 15 to 20% of the world's population live in severe absolute economic poverty, while up to 50% may be said to suffer some form of it. Although absolute economic poverty is found everywhere, most of its victims live in Africa, Asia and Latin America. According to the United Nations Food and Agriculture Organization, the four social groups most seriously affected are generally the rural landless, the urban unemployed, women and children.[10] The question I now address is whether the existence of absolute economic poverty represents an injustice. The possible injustice of relative poverty will only be briefly touched upon. It should be clear that the question of justice varies somewhat with each definition of poverty.

Criteria of Justice

The question of social justice is very complex. The language of moral analysis is by no means standard. Values underpinning the criteria of justice in contemporary society are quite pluralistic. As the recent economics pastoral of the Catholic Bishops in the United States shows, Christian tradition embodies a radically communitarian ethic (in contrast to individualism, emotivism or utilitarianism).[11] Its guiding orientation expresses general norms such as do not harm others (the ten commandments), do good to others (the beatitudes and the good Samaritan), the universal destination of all the goods of creation, the inalienable dignity of the person and the common good. Each of these notions has sparked the development of a considerable body of literature. I cannot adequately treat these issues here. Suffice it to recognize that this is the tradition out of which I am operating.

In speaking of social justice, what are the main questions which must be faced? First, in justice discourse there is an underlying question of general social equality and the legitimacy of social differences: do all persons and people deserve the same social consideration and treatment? The question is whether the absolutely poor are truly subjects of their political and economic structures and institutions or merely subject to them. This point comes into focus in terms of five more specific questions and themes which one finds recurrent in contemporary literature: dependency, emargination, deprivation, unconcern and sanctions. Each point poses a different question of general social equality. The positive content of the notion of justice can be made more specific in terms of these themes.

First, liberty versus dependence: are all persons and peoples to enjoy the same degree of liberty and self-determination? Catholic teaching affirms the rights of peoples and of individuals and groups within peoples to self-determination. In this way the freedom of the oppressed and dependent takes priority over the licentious liberty of the powerful.

Second, inequality of opportunity: are all persons and peoples to enjoy the same rights to participate in social structures? Emargination denies individuals, groups and peoples equal opportunity and the right to participate fully in political, economic and social life. Pushed to the edges of these social structures and institutions, the emarginated must endure all the duties and strictures of society without receiving any of the benefits. Church teaching affirms the right of poor and emarginated persons and peoples to participate in social structures in the face of their exclusion from these benefits by the powerful.

Third, deprivation versus equality of distribution: should all persons and people receive the same amount of resources, goods and services and of power attached to social offices? Deprivation underscores the case of those who live in indigence and cannot meet their needs on either an individual or national level, while others enjoy enormous wealth. Regarding distribution of resources, goods and services, church teaching affirms the priority of the needs of the poor over the mere wants of the rich. In its distribution of formula there are four criteria. The priority is given to needs and then to effort within a context of equal opportunity. Claims based upon meritocracy and historical privilege are also recognized but are fiercely conditioned by the common good and the moral obligation to do good. The priorities in Catholic thought are needs, effort, merit and privilege in that order. This does not preclude differences, but conditions them.

Fourth, apathy and egoism versus contribution and duty: should all persons and peoples be required to make the same effort to contribute to society's well being? The plight of the poor is often met with apathy and unconcern on the part of those who are well-off. Catholic teaching stresses the duty of all to make a contribution to society according to their abilities and finds the refusal to do so, whether deriving from egoism or apathy, an unacceptable position. There is a social duty to be responsive to the overall common good and to contribute according to ones' ability.

Finally, dissent and due process versus coercion: should all persons and people enjoy the same degree of due process regarding sanctions and incentives in social structures? Economic and political sanctions against those who break the social rules of the game can only be considered unjust if the rules of the game are themselves just. Coercive sanctions and unfair schemes of incentives which treat individuals, groups and peoples as things, as instruments for either individual, group or national self-interest, are unacceptable. In the face of unjust rules of the game, dissent is a social duty.

I now turn to apply these criteria to both the causes and the solutions to absolute poverty.

Justice and the Causes of Poverty

The ethics of poverty depends upon what one thinks are the facts of poverty. In this section I am talking about causes. If poverty is a human (rather than a divine or cosmic) injustice then human structures and institutions must produce it, there must be identifiable moral responsible agents, and better alternatives must exist. I examine poverty in terms of four causes: demography and natural resources, technology, power, and culture.[12]

It is frequently asserted that poverty is caused by the imbalance between population growth and distribution and natural resource carrying capacity. The empirical question is both crucial and formidable. For if natural resource scarcity causes poverty, then the ethics of poverty leads to discussions of lifeboat ethics, triage, and moral responsibility regarding ecology and population control. My view of the empirical data distinguishes two aspects of the population/resources question: the present and the future. In a macroeconomic sense neither Africa nor Latin America finds itself in a critical position regarding either the amount of resources or of people, each using under 25% of potential agricultural resources.[13] The future population pressure will be more serious but most experts believe that given present trends in birth rates and death rates, the situation is manageable. At the same time, regional problems of population pressure and the microeconomic prospects of particular households can be very severe indeed. Asia (particularly China, India and Bangladesh) presents a far more serious population/resources problem both now and in the future. What are the moral issues involved? Within the regions there is first an obligation to manage the natural resource base in an ecologically responsible way; this is the case both at the national as well as the household level.[14] Secondly, at both of these levels there is need for a responsible population policy. I favor a population program which is part of a public health program and also integrated into programs to enhance human resource development as part of overall economic development and growth.[15] Parents should not have children they cannot properly care for; that would be unjust both to the children and to society. Yet they are entitled to self-determination; coercive measures raise many other moral problems. I think freedom of choice both regarding limiting births as well as selection of means is a right of conscience for parents. Abortion is a special case that ethically poses the rights of the unborn living. In addition, there is also a moral case for rights to international migration, for in Catholic thought the world of creation is given to all.

There are clearly many difficult questions of justice regarding resource management, population control and international migration. But I am of the opinion there is no country which cannot be self-sufficient regarding food and the basic necessities of life. Poverty is not primarily caused by natural resource scarcity; nonetheless, it is a contributing factor. It assumes much more importance as a variable in the future, especially in the context of a desired quality of life. Here it must be remembered, though, that Christian tradition places an absolute and eternal value upon human life. The very limitation of life, let alone the means, poses a very serious question for a religion that believes in eternal life in God. It is not open to frivolous trade-offs with materialistic consumerism. Nonetheless, human life is legitimately limited by human capacity to care for that life with respect and ensure it dignity.

Scarcity is a fact. Where does it come from? While it does partially result from population/natural resource imbalances, it is my opinion that scarcity itself is primarily produced by social systems. That is why I think it must be viewed against the backdrop of technology, power and culture.

Technology also presents us with a number of formidable problems of justice. There is the issue of priorities where meeting human needs is pitted against armaments, on the one hand, and the materialist consumerism of the well-off, on the other. There is the problem of the distribution of technology and research and development funds. Things as simple as fertilizer and basic irrigation systems are beyond the reach of many of the world's poor. Finally, there is the problem of choosing the appropriate technology set, targeted not simply upon narrow economic growth but growth that reaches the poor. Few if any would question the finding that today's medium level technology could easily produce enough food to feed everyone both now and in the future (assuming present population trends). True, there is much more to learn about tropical agriculture, aquaculture and so forth. But it remains that present technology sets of both production and processing could radically transform contemporary and future population/natural resource questions.

Why don't they? Both natural resource scarcity and the scarcity of technology pose the problem of power. The focus is upon exclusion of some people by others from access to resources and technology, on the one hand, and participation in the setting of priorities and decision making, on the other. There are many obvious cases of simple power plays, where this or that individual or group closes out another. But power in a social system is far more complex and is played out in terms of organizational politics between various social agents, all of whom have some power. The participants are governments, business enterprises, households, private voluntary organizations and interest groups. They are arranged in various coalitions of social classes and large complex organizations (bureaucracies).[16] The world's indigent poor are generally emarginated from larger political and economic systems, operating primarily within local level networks of household, extended family and tribe. What needs to be examined are the rules of the game governing political participation and economic opportunity.

In addition to economic and political factors, there is also a culture of poverty. As a social syndrome, poverty represents a psycho-social trap. Popular images of the poor tend to portray them as a new version of Rousseau's noble savage, bound together by effective solidarity with one another. Yet, in distinction to the poverty caused merely by denied opportunity, the culture of poverty underlines the fact that the poor often have little solidarity among themselves. Further, they internalize their condition of poverty with the result that their effective freedom and prospects for participation are severely limited. Many of the poor do not vote or take advantage of educational opportunities. They are hooked on consumerism rather than human resource development. This has prompted many observers to speak of the necessity of conscientization among the poor and the pedagogy of the oppressed.[17] Poverty exists within a matrix of cultural values and social visions; the heart of the ethical quest is to call these into question and, in so doing, probe the legitimacy of structures and institutions.

The four main causes of poverty do present us with many issues of social injustice. It should be clear that absolute poverty is precisely a case of social responsibility, for the whole responsibility cannot be convincingly laid at the door of any one social agent or class. There are, of course, some obvious cases of unjust actions on the part of exploitive landowners, corrupt governments and even manipulative religions. The greatest challenge of a social justice analysis of poverty is to delineate the concomitant responsibility of interacting social agents who together produce the poverty syndrome. Thus, in Latin America, for example, poverty cannot be understood without grasping the social role of local elites, international geopolitics, transnational economic enterprises, the social values of a certain hybrid of Catholicism, and the poor themselves. Now a word about solutions.

Motivation and Political Will

There are many different motives for overcoming policy. Some people are motivated primarily by a sense of solidarity with the poor and a thirst for social justice. Others are moved by the new markets which more than a billion poor people would represent, if they were moved to a level of adequate well being and income. Still others see that poverty is inherently destabilizing and perceive that, if something is not done now to alleviate it, those who are well-off run the risk of losing everything in the end. All these motives can be brought to bear on program design and be helpful in forging some sort of policy coalition.

The chief obstacle to overcoming poverty today is neither scarcity of resources due to population growth, nor lack of technical capacity, but a lack of political will to do so. That is the central issue in poverty as a continuing injustice.

What then might motivate people, individually or collectively, to galvanize the political will to overcome poverty? The forging of political will is a complex social process that goes forward on many levels at once. It is shaped by great leaders and innovative elites who act as catalysts, by conscientization regarding values and overall human development, by social conflict, and by new possibilities of human community ushered in by technology and material innovations.

Injustice is found not only in the causes of poverty but also in the fact that no effective political will has materialized to overcome it. Surely a major reason is the pervading spirit of groups' egoism and the erosion of communitarian values. There is collective apathy. In addition, solutions to poverty are being undermined by the deteriorating quality of political economic institutions. Increasingly, the legitimacy of such institutions is being questioned for they systematically work against the poor. It is clear that "development" does not reach the poor. Nor will it do so without radical changes not only within existing institutions but also of them; that is, altering the rules of the game in governments, the International Monetary Fund, General Agreement on Trade and Tariff, the economic rules of property, credit and so forth.

The essential ethical message to those causing poverty is "do no harm." Do not lie, cheat and steal. Governments, business elites and churches have for a long time done just that. The more difficult aspects of social justice are found in the imperative to do good, even when one may not have caused the injustice in the first place. In such a case we are calling for all social agents to contribute to the solution. As a public policy principle, it is important to note that society-wide benefits call for society-wide sharing of the social costs, empolying both user-pay and ability-to-pay principles.

Each protagonist mentioned above represents a certain potential as well as certain deficiencies when we think of their roles regarding poverty in the world today. The dynamics of organizational politics frequently become quite complex and various forms of sanctions and incentives come into play. Prophets are stoned while the prosperity of the wicked cruelly taunts victims of injustice.

Those advocating justice in economic development are accused of being utopian. They often do not agree among themselves on the criteria of justice. Yet this level of discourse is highly important, for it alone attacks the dominant values and ideologies which form the socio-cultural base of poverty and undergird its persistance. The "realists" frequently ignore such concerns as they enunciate their preferential option for the *status quo*. They do not appeal to the dispossessed but to those in power. While many social elites follow a short term strategy of grabbing and running, a newer, long-term view is taking shape among the powerful, based upon the logic of mutual self-interest and long-term maximization of gain. In either case the gambit turns upon persuasion. Here it is clear that the persuasion going on among the dispossessed turns upon justice, and the persuasion going on among the principalities and powers turns upon self-interest.

As far as solutions go, multiple approaches must be undertaken simultaneously. First, to my mind, the primary cause of absolute poverty frequently must be laid at the door of governments. It is imperative to build up justice in the area of civil authority systems by coming to terms with national security state ideologies, wasteful spending on armaments, corruption, privileged elites that are beyond accountability, and tremendous bureaucratic inefficiencies in economic planning and administration. Similarly for international geopolitics.

Second, justice must be built up in the exchange systems by improving the qualities of markets, changing the rules regarding access to and ownership of productive resources, and instituting fair price, income and profit policies. This means getting development priorities right, focusing upon the jobless and landless, those discriminated against on the basis of race, sex or religion.

Thirdly, the role of private voluntary organizations which function as social persuasion groups regarding values and public policy must be scrutinized. The research priorities of universities, the social vision of religious groups as well as their social praxis and institutional alignments must be challenged. And so with labor organizations, consumers, interest groups and so forth.

None of this is easy for it calls for 1) a reordering of social priorities, 2) a restructuring of the economy in terms of resource control and institutional frameworks, 3) an intelligent diversification of the economy to take advantage of both short- and long-term economic advantages, and 4) forging a new set of social values based on justice for all, which would lead to building up of institutions which reflect such values.

To conclude, poverty is first and foremost a social injustice rather than mere individual or class injustice, although it also is the latter. Secondly, the injustice is located in causes of poverty but also, more importantly, in narrow self-interest, apathy and the lack of political will on the part of all participants necessary to undertake effective solutions.

Notes

[1]Valentine Handwerker, *The Modern Catholic Social Teaching on the Distribution of Superfluous Goods*, Ph.D. Dissertation, Rome, Accademia Alfonsiana, 1980.

[2]St. Paul, I. Cor. 4:7.

[3]Robert Nisbet, *History of the Idea of Progress* (New York: Basic Books, 1980).

[4]William Shakespeare, *Coriolanus*, I, ii.

[5]This vision is evident in The Lay Commission on Catholic Social Teaching and the U.S. Economy, "Towards the Future, Catholic Social Teaching and the U.S. Economy. A Lay Letter," *Catholicism in Crisis* (November, 1984), pp. 3-54.

[6]Michael Harrington, *The Other America* (New York: MacMillan, 1962). For more recent studies see Michael Harrington, *The New American Poverty* (New York: Holt, Rinehart and Winston, 1984 and Charles Murray, *Losing Ground* (New York: Basic Books, 1984).

[7]Amartya Sen, "Poor, Relatively Speaking," *Oxford Economic Papers*, 1983, 35, 2, pp. 153-169.

[8]Oscar Altimir, *The Extent of Poverty in Latin America* (Washington, D.C.: World Bank Staff Working Paper, No. 522, 1982).

[9]Abraham Maslow, *Toward A Psychology of Being* (Princeton, NJ: Van Nostrand, 1968).

[10]United Nations Food and Agriculture Organization, *The Fourth World Food Survey*, Rome, 1977.

[11]"Catholic Social Teaching and the U.S. Economy," *Origins*, 14, No. 22/23, (1984), 337-383. I discuss this in more detail in Paul Steidl-Meier, *Social Justice Ministry: Foundations and Concerns* (New York: LeJacq Publishing Co., 1984), Chapter 4.

[12]I develop this in more detail in Paul Steidl-Meier, *Poverty, Development and Socio-Economic Efficiency* (Los Angeles: Loyola Marymount University, [mimeo], 1985).

[13]United Nations Food and Agriculture Organization, "How Much Good Land is Left?" *Ceres*, (July-August, 1978), pp. 14-15.

[14]C. Dean Freudenberger, *Food For Tomorrow?* (Minneapolis: Augsburg Publishing House, 1984).

[15]Paul Steidl-Meier, *Social Justice Ministry: Foundations and Concerns* (New York: LeJacq Publishing Co., 1984), Chapter 12.

[16]Charles Lindblom, *Politics and Markets* (New York: Basic Books, 1977), part II.

[17]Paolo Freire, *The Pedagogy of the Oppressed* (New York: Continuum Books, 1970).

IV. Theological and Religious Perspectives

AN AFFLUENT AMERICAN RESPONDING TO GLOBAL POVERTY

William Wood, S.J.

On a bleak cold day in December 1966 in Wepion, Belgium, a young Congolese Brother knocked on the door of my room at the Institut Bellarmin. This was a house of formation for Jesuits and, a year-and-a-half ordained, I was pursuing "tertianship," the final year of a Jesuit's spiritual formation. Brother Konda was stopping over for a week with us, on his way back to his Jesuit community in the Belgian Congo, which has since become the Republic of Zaire.

Brother Konda's father had died recently, leaving a wife and ten children. According to African custom, the oldest son is expected to carry on the father's role as provider until the children are raised. Brother Konda was the oldest son. But he not only had left home, he had joined the Society of Jesus and taken permanent vows as a religious. What was he to do? His choice seemed to be to either find the money somehow to support the family for ten years, or to leave the order and take over his father's position as head of the family and breadwinner.

Quite briefly, what he wanted from me was $50,000 which would be about $500,000 in today's economy.

When he heard that an American Jesuit was living in the house he imagined he had stumbled into a gold mine. For, in all sincerity, Brother Konda thought all Americans were rich; he thought that I could lay my hands on $50,000 by simply making a phone call.

Such was his image of America, which had been shaped primarily by movies and news reports of politicians, movie stars, and sports figures. For him, America meant affluent, rich, rolling in wealth. And he is not alone in harboring that image.

The purpose of sharing this story with you is to try to explain why I call myself an affluent American. After all, from a technical point of view, I am poor. Because of my vow of poverty I own nothing, not even the clothes on my back. From family background and upbringing I am a combination of working class/lower middle class. But in the eyes of the people of the Third World, of Eastern Europe, and even many in Western Europe, to be American is to be affluent. The vast majority of the world's population beyond our borders who live in absolute or relative poverty, and the 35 million Americans whose income keeps them under the poverty line, regard you and me as affluent.

Whether how others perceive us is accurate or not, it is important to pay attention to their perception. For if we speak of absolute poverty and relative poverty, perhaps we can also speak of absolute and relative affluence. Relative to the vast majority of people, I am certainly affluent. Not only are all my material needs taken care of and not only do I have no worry about being provided for if I get sick or in my old age, but I have more than I need, a lot more; I live in material comfort. Compared to most people in the world and to a significant minority in this country, I am indeed affluent.

The Ideology of Affluence

But more significant in the context of responding to global poverty, is that we Americans are inexorably part of an affluent society. We are only 6 percent of the world's population, yet we use and control over 50 percent of the world's resources. We are caught up, even as part of the "American Dream," in an ideology of affluence, that happiness and human fulfillment consist in having more and more.

Affluence of itself bespeaks neither evil nor good, vice nor virtue, though Jesus warned that it is harder for a rich person to enter the Kingdom of God than a camel to pass through the eye of a needle. But I am suggesting that American society and culture is seriously afflicted with, if not dominated by, the ideology of affluence, and ideology that borders on idolatry. Eric Fromm refers to this dominant thought-pattern as the "having" mode of existence, as opposed to the "being" mode, and finds its roots in 18th century capitalism when economic behavior became separate from ethics and human values. "In the having mode of existence my relationship to the world is one of possessing and owning, one in which I want to make everybody and everything, including myself, my property." The highest goal in this ideology is to have more and more. More is better.

Underpinning the ideology of affluence are two philosophical and pseudo-ethical premises. The first is that the answer to the problem of human existence is radical hedonism, the theory that human fulfillment and well-being comes from the satisfaction of every desire. The second premise is that the pursuit of individual egoism leads to harmony and peace and even to the realization of the common good. What our society holds out as the ultimate in human living is unlimited consumption.

Very few of us would admit to radical hedonism and unlimited egoism as our philosophy of life. But my point is that we are caught up in the ideology of affluence which permeates the economic and social structures of our society. Perhaps waste is the most blatant symptom of our malady. We are so used to waste we do not even notice it. Yet visitors to the United States, especially those from poor countries, are astonished and scandalized by the waste they perceive here wherever they turn. They sense that what we *waste*, in food, fiber, water, and energy, could sustain their own countries quite adequately, if not comfortably.

But waste is only one expression of the ideology of affluence. It is further expressed by the abuse of land, the pollution of the environment, and the overdependence on fossil fuel energy, which characterizes American farming, and moved a Kentucky farmer-poet named Wendell Berry to write a book entitled *The Unsettling of America*. The lust for affluence has blinded us to the sacredness of the earth and our need as human beings to live in right relationship with nature for the sake of human life and culture. There is no room in the affluent society for gratitude in the realization that all we have, all we are, and the earth and atmosphere that sustain us are God's gifts, to be received and used lovingly and responsibly with faithful stewardship.

A society dominated by the attitude that having is more valuable than being, inevitably becomes as contemptuous of human life as it is contemptuous of nature. Being connotes all that is dynamic: living and loving life, changing, growing, caringly people-centered. Having is static: dead and choosing death, going nowhere with no one, dehumanizingly thing-centered. Things are more valuable than people in the ideology of affluence, which lusts for death: get rid of people so you can have more.

So, population control becomes the first—and, for so many

Americans, the only—response to a world of hunger. And good sincere women are so blinded by this ideology that over a million of their babies are aborted each year, 95 percent of these abortions having nothing to do with rape, incest or danger to the mother's life. Infanticide is not far off, nor is geronticide. We are becoming more aware of the incredible incidence of child abuse in our country, as well as the maltreatment and abandonment of the elderly. And is it just coincidental that recent polls indicate that 80 to 85 percent of American citizens favor the death penalty? Here we are, the most wealthy, powerful and technologically advanced nation in the history of the world, and we have not been able to prevent crime or protect our citizens from violence, so we allow ourselves to be duped into playing "let's pretend" we have a solution, by killing people. It is all part of the anti-life sickness of the ideology of affluence.

The purpose of painting this rather bleak picture of affluence is not to arouse guilt feelings. It is to pay close attention to who I am and what I am a part of as I try to respond to global poverty, and to analyze precisely what the problem is which I summarize as "global poverty."

Poverty

Reflecting on the ideology of affluence, I come to see that the "having" mode of existence is no answer to poverty. The alienation of affluence and its other dreadful effects such as increasing teenage suicide, violent crime, alcoholism and drug-addiction, sadomasochistic sex and pornography, abortion and child abuse, divorce and erosion of family values, etc., are First World symptoms of the same disease that afflicts people of the Third World in the form of absolute poverty. The abundance of material goods can be as dehumanizing and destructive as their absence.

Which brings me to a brief reflection on poverty itself. Let me suggest five points about poverty to guide our responses and, for this discussion, develop only the last point.

1. "Poverty" is a thing-word, an abstraction. We are much better off thinking about real, live people who suffer poverty and who cry out for our compassion, not just our scientific analysis. We have much to learn from Mother Teresa who sees and reflects the face of Christ in every abandoned baby

she cuddles, in every leper to whom she doles out soup, in every outcast old person she brings to her house to die in dignity.

2. The principal suffering of the poor is shame and disgrace, the feeling of being worthless, as well as powerless to determine their own lives and destinies.

3. People do not suffer chronic poverty because of overpopulation or scarcity of land and natural resources, nor because they lack technological know-how.

4. People are poor as the result of human decisions and management, inequitable power relationships, maldistribution of resources, and the cultural values which determine the human relationships which are built into economic, social and political structures.

5. Just as poverty must be confronted in its causality, so does it need to be addressed as one piece in the puzzle which is the urgent reality of our present historical situation. It is the whole of this historical reality to which I am struggling to respond. (My development of this point is drawn generously from the analysis of Father Albert Nolan in his powerful little book, *Jesus Before Christianity*.)

Global Disorder

The destitution of millions is but one of a number of life and death problems that characterize our age. These are a matter of life and death, not just for individuals or even just for whole nations and civilizations, but for the entire human race. Added to our awareness of problems that threaten the survival of mankind on this planet is our fear that there is no solution to these problems and that no one will be able to stop our headlong plunge towards the total destruction of the human species.

We stand on the brink of nuclear annihilation, whether in a nuclear war, by some freak accident, or because some madman or terrorist manages to push the button.

But destruction by nuclear weapons is only one way we could go. We are faced with new threats that some say will destroy us more certainly and inevitably than a nuclear war: wasteful and earth-destructive high technology and energy-intensive farming that deplete natural resources and pollute the environment, while rapidly rendering the family farmer extinct; and the escalation of violence and terrorism. Expanding populations could be a blessing in a world characterized by stewardship and responsible conservation of resources. But, unless we change our ways drastically, the population explosion will be a curse upon us. Any one of these problems by itself would be threatening enough to our future; taken together they spell disaster.

Meanwhile the deserts creep up on us as soil erosion increases and more and more forests are destroyed. According to G. Scwab in *Dance with the Devil*, a single Sunday edition of the New York Times eats up 150 acres of forest land.

As Father Nolan observes, there is no need to exaggerate these problems. Solutions can be found. But these solutions would require such far-reaching and dramatic changes in the values, concerns, thought-patterns and lifestyles of so many people, especially in our country, that most would brush them off as virtually impossible. Sure, we could do something really drastic about conserving the earth's resources and searching for alternative sources of energy. But who would agree to the loss of profit and the extra costs? We could adopt means of transportation and production that do not pollute the air and the rivers. We could reduce our high standard of living voluntarily by giving up all non-essentials—including our excessive use of paper. But where would we find the human or moral resources to motivate so many of us to make such fundamental changes? It is hard enough to get someone to curtail his excesses for the sake of his own health and future. What will move him to change for the sake of others, let alone to make sacrifices for the sake of the billions who have not yet been born?

But the world abounds with good willed women and men who are deeply concerned and willing to commit themselves as well as get involved. But what can one person or any number of persons do about it all? We are up against the system that has its own momentum and its own dynamics.

Now we have reached the heart of the problem. Blinded by the "having" approach to life, the world has built up an all-inclusive political and economic system, which is not only counter-productive and has brought us to the brink of disaster, but has become our master. Nobody seems to be able to change or control this system. Most frightening of all is that there is nobody at the helm and that the impersonal machine we have so carefully designed will drag us along inexorably to destruction.

This system, which Rubem Alves calls the Dinosaur, produces both wealth and poverty. Wealth is concentrated more and more in the hands of a few, while the ranks of the poor increase. As poor nations try to measure up to the standards of development and economic growth demanded by the First World dominated system, the more indebted they become, and so all the poorer. Among nations, if not within all of them, there is competition. But everyone does not in fact have an equal chance. In simplest terms, the more one has, the more he can make, and the more he can make, the less there is for those who do not have enough to compete with him. It is a vicious circle in which the poor are always the losers. Currently something like two billion people, nearly two-thirds of the human race, live in subhuman conditions with insufficient food, clothing and shelter. Hundreds of millions of people are born into this world to experience little more than the pangs of hunger and the sufferings which result from malnutrition and deprivation.

The most obscene thing about this ugly reality is that it does not have to be—we live on a bounteous earth where there is plenty for all, as long as the few know when enough is enough. We can and do continue to produce more wealth, but we have built a system incapable of ensuring that the bare necessities of life are evenly distributed. This is because it is geared to profits rather to people.

This passion for "having," built into the system, must lead to violence and war. As long as everybody wants to have more, and unlimited consumption is the goal of living, then competition becomes violence, and the building up of arms for security becomes a country's pre-eminent need. Once again a thing, national security, takes precedence over people. Apart from the institutional violence of injustice, oppression and exploitation, military governments are multiplying. Only military dictatorship can maintain the system, since institutional violence leads to revolutionary violence, which in turn leads, as in Central America and the Philippines and South Africa, to more institutional violence in the form of riot police, detention without trial, torture, marshall law and political murders. Dom Helder Camara refers to the "spiral of violence" which, if something drastic cannot be done about all the other problems (population, poverty, pollution, wastage, inflation, diminishing resources and environmental destruction), will inevitably include us all in an act of mutual destruction.

This is the context in which poverty prevails in the world today, with only worse in store for tomorrow. As Father Nolan says, there is no point exaggerating these problems for ideological purposes and yet, on the other hand, we cannot afford to ignore them. But how can we respond?

The Responses of Despair and Fatalism

Fellini's *La Dolce Vita* portrays the alienation of affluence: the sickness, boredom, and decadence of well-to-do people moving from one titillation or pleasure to another, all without meaning. Marcello Mastroianni wanders through the film searching for value. A ray of hope shines in the person of a very decent, atheistic humanist who likes to entertain in his well-furnished Roman condo. One evening, his hospitality includes a lecture on India by an eloquent world traveler. After all the guests have left that evening, the humanist host remains thoughtfully awake throughout the night. He listens over and over again to the tape of the evening's lecture, especially to the part of the tape that describes the masses of the poor of Calcutta: beggars, diseased people, abandoned infants, and old people left to die in the streets. After much reflection, the gentleman rises, goes to the closet and gets a revolver, enters the nursery and kills his two small children, and then shoots himself—free at last, and his children, too, from a fundamentally evil world where everyone is helpless to do anything about human suffering in the streets of Calcutta.

The greatest danger facing Christian social change agents today, according to Denis Goulet, is clearly the loss of hope. Despair is an increasingly common response to the world in which we live, an overwhelming sense of helplessness and hopelessness. Tristram Coffin perceives this response coming chiefly from the "most sensitive members of our society, the teenagers." The *Washington Post* reports: "American teenagers, frequently wielding parents' firearms, are killing themselves in epidemic numbers, suicide experts said. One teenage suicide every two hours, more than 6,000 in 1983, an attempt every minute, are the grim statistics. Boston psychologist Pamela Canton gives as reasons: fear of nuclear attack, increasing child abuse, alcoholism and family dissolution."[1] The *New York Times* finds that the young are "impressed" with the complexity of the problems of pollution, starving refugees, overpopulation, nuclear proliferation. "But unlike the students of the 1960s, today's undergraduates feel they have no way of addressing these problems . . . fear there is no place in the world for them..." (p. 3).

Closely allied to the response of despair is that of fatalism. "Poverty is inevitable," goes the refrain, "and anything we do to try to deal with it only makes it worse. We are powerless. It is hopeless." Fatalism easily decays, among the less well-off, into mindless violence and frustrated vandalism. Among the upwardly mobile, like the newly emerged Yuppies, fatalism degenerates into the escapist route of living in a self-centered, "get mine," fantasy world. According to *U.S. News and World Report*, "Yuppies are said to have insatiable appetites for designer clothes, video recorders, pasta makers, phone-answering devices, espresso machines, pagers and other gadgets. Volvos and BMWs are very popular. An Atlanta auto dealer reports that young adults fill a waiting list of up to 60 days for $32,000 Jaguars . . . Ambience is a must for restaurants . . . They demand cuts in government spending and seem less concerned for the poor and elderly" (p. 3).

And so, many Americans, convinced by government, big business and the media that there really is no problem, or that it is all too overwhelming and we are powerless, become victims themselves or aggravate and perpetuate the serious condition of our world by turning to the totally irresponsible and self-serving attitude that lies at the root of our global disorder.

Response of Hope

But in the midst of this dark, storm-filled world the sun is shining. Throughout the masses of suffering humankind there are peaceful, smiling, hopeful faces. Americans cannot and do not have to save the poor. We need to get off their backs, to remove obstacles that prevent them from taking charge of their own lives and destinies. We need to stop bolstering and funding governments that oppress their people and corporations that exploit the poor. We need to stop being the leading arms' merchant of an overarmed planet. But only hungry people will overcome world hunger; only the poor will undo the shackles of poverty, if we get out of the way and free ourselves of the ideology of affluence which is destroying us.

What is good news is that people all over the world are thinking and living in a radically hopeful manner that runs directly counter to the destructive ideology of affluence. Signs of hope, people self-lessly working in solidarity, can be found in Brazil and Central America, in Asia and Africa and throughout the world. A Mother Teresa has brought hope to and illuminated the human beauty to be found in the streets of Calcutta, just as Lech Walesa stands as a beacon of solidarity in Eastern Europe, and a Desmond Tutu proclaims hope even in South Africa. And here in the United States, there are thousands of people of all ages, but especially the young, who are saying "no" to the ideology of affluence and "yes" to people; "no" to star wars and military buildup, "yes" to concern for the poor and redesigning an economy as if people matter. We see this counter-cultural hope in the Sanctuary movement, the Peace movement, the Environmental movement, and the protest against apartheid in South Africa. We sense the hopeful impact of thousands of individuals exercising responsible Christian citizenship as members of Bread for the World, Network, the American Friends Service Committee, Interfaith Action for Economic Justice and others. We feel the challenge and promise of the Spirit in dedicated simple-lifestyle and prophetic communities such as the Sojourners. And then there are the countless young people who give up a year or years of their lives in volunteer service, not least of whom are those in the Jesuit Volunteer Corps.

Let me highlight five characteristics of those who are in the process of changing the world.

1. *Compassion*: Quite simply, like Jesus, they are awakened and driven by compassion—a compassion that sometimes expresses itself as tender care and concern and sometimes comes out as righteous anger denouncing injustice.

2. *Conversion*: Moved by compassion, the effective world-changer undergoes *metanoia*, repentance, a radical change of thinking and mindset. Conversion involves an awakening to one's own self-worth and the value of each human person, accompanied by the realization that people are neither helpless nor powerless once they recognize and accept their true identity, worth, origin, and destiny.

3. *Community*: The call to metanoia makes a person more aware of his or her own sinfulness and need for healing, as well as the need to love and be loved, to support and be supported, to follow through one's conversion in union and solidarity

with others. Conversion makes a person more conscious of the human community and the realization that we cannot responsibly become the global village community, unless we are in communion on the local level in which we live and act out that which we are working toward. Inescapably, if not always consciously, such community is religious, a creative communion of family members reunited by the death of their Brother and animated by His Spirit to walk justly and lovingly as sons and daughters of the living God in whose image they were created. This is the discovery of real power.

4. *Critical Thinking*: Simplistic and naive responses can do more damage than good. The effective participant in the reshaping of society will never be satisfied with easy answers or facile solutions. Reading, studying, meditating, talking with people, seeking the right questions, engaging in systematic social analysis, and devising effective plans and strategies for action, there is never a time when this task is completed. In a rapidly changing and very complex world, there is a continuing demand for reflective analysis and revision of what we are doing in terms of that analysis.

5. *Sustained Commitment*: This may be the very hardest part for Americans. We want instant solutions. We need to learn the wisdom of the Far East, which knows how to be patient. We need to learn the truth of I.F. Stone's statement that if you find an answer to your question in your lifetime, you are not asking a big enough question.

Anything worthwhile takes time, not just hours or days, but years, decades, centuries. So, take a deep breath and relax. It took centuries to get the world in the mess it is in. We are not going to redo the whole thing overnight or even in our lifetime. But we are going to redo it.

Those who effectively shape the world of tomorrow for the better are men and women driven by compassion who undergo conversion to new ways of thinking and being and acting. They think critically and carry on the task with sustained commitment, strengthened by a community of living faith, working in collaboration and coalition toward the day when the human community will be restored to the image of God, each person living in dignity and the full relationship of unconditional love with every other person.

I can tell you that things will not just happen. The world will be shaped by those who wake up and choose to shape it. I intend to be part of that shaping. And you can, too.

It will take our lifetime and beyond. So let us get on with it.

Note

[1]As quoted in *The Washington Spectator*, ed. Tristram Coffin, 11, No. 4 (February 15, 1985), 3. All further references to this work appear in the text.

POVERTY AND CONSCIENCE

Robert McAfee Brown

I want to begin with some comments about those two basic words, "conscience" and "poverty," because both of them evoke many different kinds of definitional response. Let me refresh your minds by indicating some of the dictionary definitions of "conscience."

Frequently there is a very positive definition of conscience: "a knowledge or sense of right and wrong with a compulsion to do right." Sometimes there is another kind of definition: "a moral judgment that opposes the violation of a previously recognized ethical principle and that leads to feelings of guilt if one violates such a principle." (I think that one must have been written by a Protestant.)

So, on the one hand, "conscience" represents a compulsion to do right, and on the other hand, a sense of guilt when one does wrong, knowing all the time what "doing right" would mean. We see this at work when we talk about someone who is a "conscientious objector"—one who makes a decision not to do what the public law demands, and feels strongly enough about it to be willing to break the law if the law demands doing something which in conscience seems wrong. This has been very clear in the last couple of decades in the United States, illustrated by people who say, "In conscience, I cannot go to war." They have claimed allegiance to a higher law then the law of the state, which they have called the law of conscience.

This has made the government very unhappy, and during the 60s, when this was a burning personal issue—when every male on every campus and every female who knew a male on campus discovered it was not just a theoretical issue—the government tried in every way it could to make it extremely difficult for individuals to act out of conscience. The penalties for refusing to serve in the military were up to five years in jail and a $10,000 fine. And if, to avoid that, a potential draftee went to Canada, there was no assurance that the individual would ever be allowed to return.

It is becoming even more of an issue today. The recent indictments of people who have been giving sanctuary to political refugees from El Salvador and Guatemala, is focusing the issue of conscience once more, because in the upcoming trials the government is going to argue that no evidence should be admissible. That argues that church people were sheltering refugees out of conscience, or out of religious motivation, or out of a sense of moral outrage at what our government was doing in shipping the political refugees back to likely death. So we are going to have increasing attention given to the issue of the rights of conscience in relation to the claims of the state.

So as I use this word, I will be thinking of conscience as kind of a voice within us that, in the light of some of society's accepted standards and criteria for action, says "wait a minute," and insists on examining the conflict which an individual has moral qualms about doing what society prescribes, and tries to come to an informed conclusion.

The adjective "informed" is very important. Our word "conscience," comes from *conscientia*, which contains the verb *scio* which means to know." That is to say, conscience is not just whim, it has to do with knowing, knowing as much as we can about what we are doing, so that our conclusion is an informed conclusion, making as much use as possible of the tools of our minds. That is part of it. But in addition it means not only examining the issue and coming to an informed conclusion, but being willing to *act* on the basis of that conclusion. This means a willingness to take sides on an issue of public debate. Very often it will mean taking sides against the majority, and if we do not have this final ingredient of the willingness to take sides and act, we will end up with a flawed conscience which comes to the point of decision and then tries to back away.

The real betrayal under such circumstances, may not be so much taking the wrong side as attempting to avoid taking sides. I do not think it is possible to take a neutral stance when an issue of conscience is raised, for whoever says "I am not going to decide," has in fact already decided to support by default whoever has the greater power in a given situation. And whoever has the greater power can only rejoice when someone says "I am not going to make a decision, I am going to sit this one out, I am going to be neutral." We saw this graphically half a century ago when the so-called "good Germans" wanted to remain neutral on the Nazi party's attitude toward the Jews. They said things like, "The issue is very complex," or, "The government must have good reasons for wanting to get rid of the Jews," or "We do not have all the facts yet, we can't yet act," or "There is surely truth on both sides of the question, so we won't make a judgment." We know all these. I think it is clear that such people were not being "neutral;" they were supporting the government policy of seeking to exterminate all Jews. And that kind of assessment is necessary when we talk about poverty by complaining, "How are we going to deal with the issue of poverty, it is really much too complicated" or insist that it really is not a problem. The *San Jose Mercury News* carried a column a couple of weeks ago by a Roman Catholic layman who was dealing with the statistic that there are 35 million people below the poverty level in the United States—a fact that appalled the Roman Catholic bishops but did not appall him. He argued that there really is not a problem, because it is not the *same* 35 million people who are poor all the time. People are always coming in and out of the poverty situation, he argued, and a lot of people go through it for a little while, and they emerge. Inescapable conclusion: do not worry, do not lose any sleep, do not let your conscience be troubled about 35 million people below the poverty level.

When one argues in such fashion, it seems to me that one has opted against the poor, from the side of the well-to-do who need not worry about the fact that a lot of people do not have the where-withal for a minimally human existence.

I have always liked a statement in the massive *Church Dogmatics* of Karl Barth, who in talking about taking sides makes the statement: "Better something overbold, and therefore in need of forgiveness, than nothing at all." Barth is saying that in moments of indecision we cannot indefinitely back away. We have to make a decision. We will make as informed a decision as we can, which might be wrong, but better to get into the struggle and learn within us than to presume that one can prescind from it when we actually cannot.

Conscience, we might put it in other terms, is the voice of that part of each one of us that still believes in justice. Without going into a lot of definitional business about justice, let me start with the traditional definition of Aristotle—that justice is giving each person his or her due—but improve on it by saying that in the interlocked world in which we live, if we really want to talk about justice and where the concerns of conscience should be pushing us, we have to talk about a world in which every *child* has his or her due. To the degree that a social policy or a political platform is so constructed that it makes provisions for every child to have what should be coming to him or her, we are getting closer than ever before to a just society.

In this light, poverty is a denial of justice, an expression of injustice. If a child (or any person) does not have the resources to live a fully human life and has to live at a subhuman level, injustice is being done to that person. So we cannot talk about conscience or poverty without talking about justice.

Now let us examine the other pole in this discussion, which is even more difficult to define with precision, what we mean when we talk about poverty.

In the Catholic tradition, with its emphasis on the vows of poverty, chastity, and obedience, it is clear that poverty, in some sense at least, is a virtue. And if you are able to think of poverty as a virtue, then it is not too hard to stop worrying about the poverty around you; somehow it has virtuous qualities attached to it. You may not decide to make poverty a virtue in your own life, but there are those who do, and when they do, three cheers for them, and poverty must somehow be good, or it would not be one of the great evangelical virtues.

So there is some confusion there. In trying to break through it, let me distinguish three kinds of poverty distinctions and borrow from Gustavo Gutiérrez, who has done the most significant work in this area. Gutiérrez talks first about *material poverty*, which has a fairly obvious meaning: the lack of sufficient economic goods for a fully human life. That is a sub-human condition, and material poverty must always be opposed. One can never make a case that it is good for people to be victims of material poverty.

It gets complicated again, when reference is made (as is so often made in the Christian tradition) to *spiritual poverty*, understood by Gutiérrez as an interior attitude of unattachment to the goods of this world, when one has achieved sufficient spiritual discernment to be able to say, "I am not going to be dependent on a lot of material goods, and I am not going to dedicate my life to getting them." But as Gutiérrez points out, this can lead to "comforting and tranquilizing conclusions." The reason should be clear: if we really persuade ourselves that we are not too attached to material goods, then it is all right to have them so long as they do not dominate our lives; if we are not too attached to them, all is well. And if there happen to be other people who have very few material goods to start with, they too can practice spiritual poverty just like we do, even in the midst of material poverty. But the biblical understanding of poverty describes it as a scandalous condition. Whenever material poverty is involved there are conditions inimicable to human dignity and therefore contrary to the will of God.

The Bible also can speak of poverty as a spiritual childhood, a sense of not being dependent on one's own pride or one's ability to gain or consume, and really to be willing always to trust in God. The Bible makes clear that the poor are blessed. Recall that strange statement in the Beatitudes: "Blessed are you poor, for you shall inherit the kingdom of God." But this is not stated to condone material poverty; it is pointing out that someday the injustice of poverty will be overcome. Gutiérrez says, commenting on that beatitude; this means the elimination of the exploitation and poverty that prevent the poor from being fully human. This has begun. The kingdom of justice which goes even beyond what people could have hoped for has begun—this is what Jesus is announcing in the Sermon on the Mount. The poor are "blessed" because the coming of the kingdom will put an end to their poverty by creating a world of brotherhood and sisterhood.

What Gutiérrez concludes from all this is that Christians must have a kind of double attitude about poverty: a commitment of both solidarity and protest. We are called to solidarity with the poor as a protest against poverty, which is a very important distinction for our own reflection. It means we are not to be tempted to glorify or romanticize poverty, that we are to deal with it by acts of identification with, and solidarity with, the poor.

Now that is a pretty tough assignment, especially for middle-class people like ourselves. And probably the most difficult and presumptuous thing is for people who are not poor to think responsibly about what it would mean to engage in solidarity with the poor. Let me take the risk of trying to open that up a bit.

First of all, I suggest that we can sharpen our consciences on this issue if we think not so much of the concept of poverty, as something that ought to be overcome, but of the existence of poor people as something that must be overcome. It is relatively easy to dispose of a concept or an intellectual formulation. We need to think in as much personalized terms as possible.

So we are talking about the reality of poor persons, persons who have been created in God's image and given the potential of dignity, but in whom, because of their poverty, that image of God has been sadly defaced in them, and for whom the possibility of full human dignity is no longer present. Thinking of poor persons, then, the task of an informed conscience is to seek ways in which the material poverty that destroys them can be removed and their dignity as persons can be restored. This means enabling them to play a role in creating their own destinies rather than having those destinies determined by someone else.

One of the greatest problems in dealing with the poverty in the United States is that one administration tends to think not of poor persons who suffer, but of poverty as a statistic that can be quantified. As long as anyone can de-personalize the matter by reducing persons to statistics, one can argue (as we have already seen) that the poverty level is not as scandalous as it first appeared, and that we have matters pretty well under control.

So if we are going to take seriously the notion of an informed conscience, let us not escape into concepts or theories of poverty; let us try to keep before us the faces of poor persons.

Secondly, it is important that people like ourselves recognize the impossibility of truly understanding, much less to entering into, the plight of poor people. Let us always make the attempt, but let us also realize there is something phony when those whom Marie Augusta calls the "non-poor" assume they can really internalize the plight of the poor. I do not say that judgmentally as much as descriptively. I simply cannot speak for the poor, and most of us who read books like this cannot do so either.

This fact was brought home to me powerfully about 10 years ago when my wife and I were in South Africa. We had a chance to talk with Steve Biko, who was later murdered by the white government because he was too much of a threat as a potential black African leader. He was initially very cool if not curt with us. Why should he tell us what it was like to be a South Africa black, on the assumption that we could interpret his situation back home, when we could never truly understand it? It seemed as though the conversation had ended before it really began. And then my wife said to him, "I think I know what you mean. When a man says, 'Let me tell you what women think,' I get very angry." A smile came over Steve Biko's face because she understood his plight, and he realized she could be trusted not to falsify the testimony. Henry Nouwen makes the point powerfully in the account of his trip to Latin America, entitled *Gracias*, in which he was struggling to live a life of spirituality in the midst of terrible material poverty in Ciudad de Oros, an horrendous collection of shacks that had sprung up over night on the outskirts of Lima. He was very honest in acknowledging that he could survive there only because now and then he could go back. He can go back to the Maryknoll headquarters, shower, have a decent meal, see a movie, and talk with other priests. He realized that if he really got sick, the support systems around him would not let him stay in Ciudad de Oros, he would be brought out, given good hospital care, and would probably recover. He understood that he could not enter into that situation in any kind of total way; he always had escape routes open to him. So, let us retain some restraint in claiming to know too much about poverty, or assuming that we can really understand how poor people feel.

With that in mind, let us examine the kinds of motivations we bring to the issue of relating conscience and the reality of poverty, or as we have suggested, the relation of conscience and the reality of poor persons.

There is an old Protestant adage that goes: *guilt* will see us through; if we just feel guilty enough, maybe we will do what needs to be done. It may be that guilt can create a little initial sensitizing, but in the long run, and probably in the short run as well, guilt is a very poor motivation. When we become involved out of a sense of guilt, it is not necessarily to help people in trouble, but because we want to get some guilt off our backs, or score a few points on the positive side of the ledger, or just plain feel good. To operate out of a sense of guilt ignores two things: (a) that we are still locked in ourselves; and (b) that no amount of good works will finally remove guilt; only forgiveness can do that.

A second kind of motivation for the arousal of conscience is *anger* (a real no-no in my liberal Protestant upbringing). Something is lacking in a conscience that is not outraged at the conditions under which poor people have to live in the world today. People should be outraged when the non-poor will not acknowledge the reality of those conditions.

We should be outraged at the spectacle of a well-fed Edwin Meese telling the American people that hunger in the United States is only an "anecdotal" issue, and that there is no "hard data" to show that hunger exists. And we should be doubly outraged that a man with that perspective can become Attorney General of the United States. This has nothing to do with the fact that he is a Republican; but it has everything to do with the fact that as the highest judicial officer in the land he now administers a system that is already skewed toward the rich and against the poor, and does so from a perspective that says, "There are not really any hungry people around, that is just a lot of gossip." That is bad news for the cause of justice. Without making him the scapegoat, let us agree that trying to ignore an issue like poverty ought to outrage us all.

There is a difference between anger and hatred. I am not talking about hatred, which is always destructive, because it deals with persons in ways that destroy personhood. But unlike hatred, anger can be channeled creatively. It can energize us to try to change the conditions that produce the realities that anger us. Surely something is wrong if we are not angry at the fact that two-thirds of the human family goes to bed hungry every night, or that in our own country there are 35 million people below the poverty level.

Juan Luis Segundo, a Jesuit from Uruguay, gives us a good starting point for these concerns. It goes very simply: "the world should not be the way it is." If you are satisfied with the way the world is, he says, then you have no idea what we are trying to do in the Third World. And if you really believe "the world should not be the way it is,"—a world in which the few who have most of the goods and the many have few of them—and if you are not somehow angered by that reality and determined to channel that anger in the direction to change, then something is wrong.

There is a verse in Psalm 4 that encapsulates all this in just six words, and the first three are a lot easier to understand than the last three. The psalmist throws off the phrase: "Be ye angry and sin not." We have some pretty good ideas about how to be angry, but how to be angry without sinning . . . that is another proposition. I think it means at least that we are sinning if our anger is directed at people only for the purpose of trying to destroy them.

Another kind of motivation springs from compassion. The word is stronger than it sounds, being derived from *cum-passio*, meaning "to suffer with," to stand alongside the one in need. Compassion is an attitude of identification with the other, an act of solidarity. Although we can never fully achieve that (as we saw earlier) we can at least work toward it, for to the degree that we can even begin to be alongside the other in the struggle against poverty, we can begin to create forces for change.

Another motivation when confronting the reality of poor persons is charity, "doing things" for others. Who can look at the evening news, with a first-hand report of starvation in Ethiopia, and not feel a genuine desire out of charity, to get food to people? I do not want to put that down; I want only to insist (as a transition to an even sounder motivation) that it is not enough to invoke charity after the fact. That may effect a momentary alleviation of the suffering, but if we are content to do no more than provide food each day, so that the people do not starve, we are not getting to the root of the problem: why is there starvation in the first place?

We have to begin asking about the reasons for the starvation. How much of it has to do with the climate? How much of it has to do with the abuse of the soil through unintelligent planting patterns? How much of it has to do with other nations refusing to share the surplus grain that is rotting in their warehouses? How much of it has to do with trade patterns that keep Ethiopia poor while other nations prosper?

This is another way of saying that being a good Samaritan is not enough. Project beyond Jesus' story for a minute. Suppose the Samaritan goes down to Jericho the next week and finds another person who has been beaten up by robbers. The chances are that he will pick that person up too, and bind the wounds, and secure what further medical aid is necessary. But when he goes down the following week and there are two people there, and the next time the victim is dead—sooner or later it is going to occur to him that his charity is coming too late, that his responses are inadequate, and that it is not enough just to pick up the pieces and have plenty of band-aids on hand.

Obviously the band-aids are needed, but they do not deal with the heart of the problem. Some more questions are in order:

Why are people being mugged on the road from Jerusalem to Jericho? Is it related to the recent rise in unemployment? Are wages so low that people cannot make a living and have to moonlight by holding up strangers? What has this got to do with the structure of a society in which enough people have to be out of work so that "uppity" robbers will realize that if they do not like their wages there are plenty of others willing to take over their jobs?

Here we need to introduce a term that has only begun to gain currency in the theological/ethical world, although the reality it describes has been around a long time. The term is systemic evil, the evil inherent in the very structures of society. We are learning that there are not poor people because here and there an evil person is trying to do them in. Things are more complex than that. It is more likely to be the case that there are a lot of good people around, acting with the best of intentions, who may, even in carrying out those intentions, do tremendous damage to other people.

No member of a board of directors on a corporation says; "Let us find a way to make more profits so that children will starve." But it is that person's obligation to say, "Let us find a way to make more profits . . ." And what is tragic is that the unintended consequence of trying to make more profits might be that some children will starve. For example, if the company decided to acquire land in Central America and start a coffee plantation, that might make good sense as a high profit long-term investment. But in the process, dozens of small farms, where people have raised enough food for their families are taken over and no more food can be raised on them. The coffee is planted, and while there may be magnificent coffee crops, the people who used to live there and work the land cannot eat coffee, or feed coffee to their children, even if they are working on the coffee plantation, they may not be making enough wages from the company to buy the food that their children need. So their children become victims of malnutrition at best, and starve at worst. Simultaneously, the coffee plantation is doing well and providing a handsome profit for the stockholders in Larchmont and Marin County.

That is not just a fabricated situation; it illustrates the kind of dynamics that happen repeatedly. The reality is that, with the best will in the world and with no intention to do harm, people are caught within structures that may do grievous harm to other people of whose existence they are not even aware. That is the kind of deeper analysis we need to undertake.

To conclude, let me say a word about the kind of responses the church can make to the reality of poor persons. This issue is being directly and helpfully addressed by the first draft of the bishops' letter on the economy. In this letter the bishops are trying to identify the root causes of poverty.

"Our perspectives and our conclusions," they wrote, "are shaped by an overriding concern for the impact of decisions and policies on the lives of people, especially the poor. Our fundamental norm is this: *will this decision or policy help the poor and deprived*

*members of the human community and enable them to become more active
participants in economic life?*"[1]

Both the points in the italicized portion are important. (1) Will
the decision help the poor and deprived members of the human
community? And even more important, (2) will it enable them to
become more active participants in economic life?

The bishops avoid the trap of saying, "We ought to do good
things for these people," an attitude that would still leave the poor
less than human, because they would not be making the decisions
about their own destiny. Instead, the bishops are saying that we
need structures in our economic life that will enable the poor to
take part themselves in the creation of their own futures.

That is going to be very difficult for the rest of us who will have
to pull back a little, in order to make that possible. The bishops
insist that the church must make "a preferential option for the
poor," which does not mean an exclusive option for the poor, as
though nobody else mattered. It means that if we are concerned
about "liberty and justice for all" we do not begin by saying, "Let us
make a preferential option to the rich, and if they are rich enough,
some of that wealth will trickle down to the poor." Rather, we begin
by creating structures in which the poor will no longer be poor.
And that will be a step on the road to creating a society where
justice—everyone getting his or her due—will be a greater possibility.

What would it mean for us to make "a preferential option for
the poor?" We need to avoid the notion that it is our task to do
things for them, as though it is enough for them to be the recipients
of our largesse, usually given in a patronizing manner. Let me get at
the alternative by examining a phrase about the Church that has
had considerable currency. It can be found in World Council documents, and in many speeches of John Paul II. It describes the task
of the church as being "the voice of the voiceless."

There is something appealing about that: those who cannot
speak, can learn that there is someone ready to speak for them. But
on further reflection I have come to feel that it is not adequate and
may even be counterproductive, because it can as easily become
patronizing. Rather than talking about the Church as the voice of
the voiceless, perhaps we should begin to talk about the Church as
the place where the voiceless can acquire a voice of their own, where
they can begin to speak for themselves, and where they can consequently be empowered.

The scriptures speak about this concern for the poor all the time. Try going through some of the passages that are familiar to you, listening to what they say about the poor, and it is astonishing how omnipresent the message is. The simplest encapsulation is Jesus' agenda for his ministry, which he announces in Nazareth, (Luke 4:16-30). He did not make it up; he got it from Isaiah 61 and claimed it for himself. What are his concerns? Things like liberty for the oppressed, freedom for the captive, good news *to the poor*. Jesus made that agenda pretty clear, and our central task today is to recover for ourselves some of the urgency that it had for him.

Note

[1]"Catholic Social Teaching and the U.S. Economy," *Origins*, 14, No. 22/23 (1984), 381.

THE CATHOLIC CHURCH
AND THE POOR

Francis R. Smith, S.J.

In 1968, at Medellín, Colombia, the Second Conference of the Bishops of Latin America committed the Catholic Church in Latin America to an "option for the poor." The consequences of that decision continue to reverberate, not merely in Latin America but throughout the Catholic Church. This essay will try to provide the reader with a context in which to understand this historic turn in Latin American Catholicism, and secondly, the continuing attempt by the *magisterium* (the teaching authority) of the Church to evaluate that decision. I will do this by concentrating on the debate over a key sentence endorsed by the 1971 Synod of Bishops. My survey will cover this debate through the 1984 document of the Congregation for Divine Faith, "Instruction on Certain Aspects of the 'Theology of Liberation.'"

On the eve of Vatican II, John Courtney Murray wrote an essay called "Is It Basket Weaving?"[1] The "It" in the title was life, existence, and by extension, Christian existence. Murray was recalling an early form of Christian existence, that of the monks of the desert. The story goes that in the morning the monk would weave a basket. In the afternoon he would unweave it. The next day he would start over. The image is transparent. True Christian existence is a patient waiting for the world to come. This world is passing away. Nothing done here has lasting value. Let us turn from the illusory seductions of this world. Let us live in patient hope, uninvolved in a fallen world, waiting for salvation. Murray called this "eschatological Christianity."

Murray pointed out that in the history of Christian existence there was a strong counter-trend. He called this "incarnational

Christianity." Here the arena of Christian existence was not the desert but the city. The "incarnational" Christian took the world seriously, affirmed its value. Sometimes the "incarnational" Christian overvalued the world. A sacred canopy was draped over contingent worldly realities, wars, politics, philosophy. Individuals claimed divine commissions to govern, and nations claimed they were God's chosen instruments for the salvation of history.

Murray thought these two tendencies, the eschatological and the incarnational, were both part of an authentic Christianity. True Christian existence did not eliminate either but held them in tension. His own judgment was that, in the period called modern history, Christianity as a whole, but especially Roman Catholicism, had been in an eschatological period, at least as compared to its medieval form. He anticipated and urged a new engagement of Christianity with a now "secularized" world, a movement of Christianity toward a more incarnational stance in order to redress what he believed to be an imbalance.

It is not an oversimplification to say that Vatican II was, as such, an attempt to make the Church and its message relevant to the world. "*Aggiornamento*," updating, but also engagement, relevance, effectiveness, incarnation, were its program. Many Catholics thought this was a novelty, even a dangerous novelty. It has its dangers, but it was not a novelty. The separation of religion from culture is a recent phenomenon. Indeed, what Vatican II was calling for was a resumption of the traditional role of Christianity as a leaven of culture. In the modern age a process has occurred called secularization. An emancipation of humanism from its Christian origins has taken place. The division of Christianity in the sixteenth century removed a common basis for culture and society, with the result that religion turned inward. Concepts originally rooted in the Gospel, the concepts of law, freedom, conscience, and their incarnation in structures, sought a new non-religious, or even anti-religious incarnation.

For a long time the Church saw the danger of the trend, not only to itself but to western culture. But it would see only one solution: restoration, return to the pre-modern synthesis of religion and culture. This led, especially in the nineteenth century, to a war between Catholicism and modernity, to a retreat of the Church within walls, to a Catholicism concerned about preserving its identity rather than a Catholicism performing its age-old role of sowing the seeds of the Gospel in the culture of its time.

Vatican II was a wrenching return to the Church's historic role vis-à-vis the world. The autonomy of the natural order, the sacredness of individual conscience, on the one hand, but on the other, the origin of the world in God, the rootlessness of values without God, the self-destructiveness of a humanism without any genuine absolute—Vatican II struggled toward an affirmation of the world and the contribution that it needs from the Gospel to be truly itself.

Under the inspiration of Vatican II and the situation of their people, the bishops of Latin America, in 1968 at Medellin, Colombia, presented salvation itself as liberation—from all sorts of oppression. They made the historic "option for the poor," which sought to overcome the "flight-from-the-world" character of much Catholic piety and to examine the implications of the Gospel for the transformation of the situation of Third World peoples. This vision came to Rome in the minds and hearts of some Latin American bishops, encountered similar thinking among some First World theologians, and found its way into the Catholic magisterial tradition in the Synod of 1971. The key, and controversial statement, of the 1971 Synod reads:

> Action on behalf of justice and participation in the transformation of the world fully appear to us as a constitutive dimension of the preaching of the Gospel, or in other words of the Church's mission for the redemption of the human race and its liberation from every oppressive situation.[2]

The history of the "reception" of this statement in the magisterium presents a fascinating story. The controversy centers on the meaning of the word "constitutive."

In a recent article, "Action for Justice as Constitutive of the Preaching of the Gospel: What Did the 1971 Synod Mean?," Charles Murphy of the North American College in Rome has provided some valuable information about what some key figures at the 1971 Synod thought "constitutive" meant.[3] The sentence was contained in the introduction to the draft document presented to the bishops by the Pontifical Commission Justice and Peace. It was written by Vincent Cosmao, O.P. According to Cosmao it was intended to convey that the preaching of the Gospel "occurs" by means of action on the behalf of justice. Or, as Murphy interprets Cosmao: "the Gospel itself, taken against its Old Testament background, is the proclamation of the intervention of God for the realization of justice."[4]

Juan Alfaro, S.J., who wrote Chapter 2 of the document, admits "constitutive" is probably not a good term because of the danger of "reducing" the Gospel to nothing but social action. Yet he does not think just any synonym will do. He does not think "integral" is strong enough to capture what was meant. He prefers the term "essential" for it avoids reducing the Gospel to nothing but action on behalf of justice but does not allow one to see such action as merely an external consequence of the preaching of the Gospel. Philip Land, S.J., also a member of the Pontifical Commission Justice and Peace, agrees that "integral" is not strong enough to capture what was meant. The point seems to be to include temporal liberation within evangelization but not reduce evangelization to temporal liberation, to say that liberation is of the essence of the Gospel but not its essence without remainder. Another influential figure in 1971 was Bishop Ramón Torrella Cascante, auxiliary of Barcelona, Vice President of the Pontifical Commission. Before the 1974 Synod he expressed the view that "constitutive" meant "integral part." He explained "integral part" as meaning not "essential" but "something which accompanies, but need not be present." Before the 1974 Synod, he believed that "strictly speaking, a true proclamation of the Gospel could take place without action for justice."[5]

Of extreme importance in this development was the attitude of the pope of the time, Paul VI. Despite the authoritative character of the synodal form of deliberation, Paul VI never made this synod's key statement his own by quoting or even paraphrasing it. When he called the next synod, in 1974, which would discuss evangelization, he set it the task of clarifying the presentation of salvation as liberation. It is important to note that a major figure at this synod was Karol Cardinal Wojtyla, archbishop of Cracow, Poland, the future John Paul II. As *relator* of the theological part of the discussion, it was his job to summarize the drift of the debate.[6] In his summary Wojtyla distinguished three positions. Some bishops, mostly from the Third World, stressed a *temporal* liberation, while others, mostly from the First and Second Worlds, stressed an *eschatological* liberation, the liberation of man through faith from the conditions of sin and mortality, the resurrection of the dead. But he pointed out that there were also bishops from the Third World who "strongly, even polemically" stressed the eschatological dimension. Wojtyla agreed with the latter. He confirmed this in his concluding summary. "Concerning the bond between liberation and the Gospel some think that the effort to liberate men is bound with the essence of the Gospel; others consider it a sign of the credibility of the Gospel . . . finally others consider the effort for comprehensive development as a fruit of the virtue of love of neighbor."[7] Wojtyla said his personal belief was that the relationship was best expressed in this third formula.

The bishops of the 1974 Synod could not agree on the linkage between faith and justice. They delivered their proceedings to Paul VI and asked him to speak for them. The result was a lengthy "apostolic exhortation," *Evangelii Nuntiandi* (1975), which is now the fundamental statement on the question in Roman Catholicism. This document stresses that the very *raison d'etre* of the Church is evangelization, the proclamation of the Kingdom of God and his salvation which is liberation from everything that oppresses men and women but is above all liberation "from sin and the evil one." But the Gospel is not merely the announcement of the forgiveness of sins and the promise of resurrection. Rather, evangelization is seen as "a complex process made up of varied elements: the renewal of humanity, witness, explicit proclamation, inner adherence, entry into the community, acceptance of signs, apostolic initiative."[8] Paul VI divided evangelization into primary and secondary elements. Primary is the proclamation of God, revealed by Jesus Christ in the Holy Spirit, his love for the world and his offer of salvation. Secondary, without which evangelization would not be "complete," are the proclamation of the rights and duties of every human being, family life, life in society, international life, peace, justice and development. Charles Murphy points out that if 1971 Synod's "constitutive" is to be interpreted by 1975 document, a good synonym for constitutive would be "essential," because the 1975 document includes action on behalf of justice as an element, even if not the primary element, in the very proclamation of the Good News and did not merely see it as an ethical consequence of the Gospel. What Murphy fails to point out is that, in fact, Paul VI, in *Evangelii Nuntiandi*, did use the word Murphy prefers. In #17 the Pope points out that in the past the Church saw evangelization in a narrow sense: proclaiming Christ to those who did not know him, preaching, catechesis, baptizing. But this is not sufficient today. All the "essential" elements must be present, those coming from the 1974 Synod in reliance on key documents of Vatican II, *Lumen Gentium*, *Gaudium et Spes*, *Ad Gentes*. Paul VI summarizes these elements in the following way: "For the Church, evangelizing means bringing the Good News into all the strata of humanity, and through its influence transforming humanity from within and making it new . . ." This takes place through an "interior change" affecting "personal and collective consciences of people, the activities in which they engage, and the lives and concrete milieux which are theirs" (#18). What is envisaged is a transformation of men and women, not in an individualistic, isolated sense, but in all their relationships, in their culture and the structures of their culture.

Lest anyone be tempted to "reduce" the Gospel to a purely temporal message, Paul VI warned that the salvation announced by the Gospel is not a purely temporal salvation—it is "transcendent and eschatological" (#27). But "evangelization would not be complete if it did not take account of the increasing interplay of the Gospel and of man's concrete life, both personal and social. This is why evangelization involves an explicit message, adapted to the different situations constantly being realized, about the rights and duties of every human being, about family life without which personal growth and development is hardly possible, about life in society, about international life, peace, justice and development—a message especially energetic today about liberation" (#29). "The Church . . . has the duty to proclaim the liberation of millions of human beings, many of whom are her own children—the duty of assisting the birth of this liberation, of giving witness to it, of ensuring that it is complete. This is not foreign to evangelization" (#30).

For Paul VI, action on behalf of justice, liberation, is included in evangelization, essential to it, even if it is its "secondary" element. It is not merely a consequence of it. If the secondary elements are not present, it is the proclamation of the Gospel that is incomplete, not merely men and women's response to it. When Karol Wojtyla became John Paul II, then, he found an authoritative word about the meaning of evangelization that contradicted his 1974 opinion. How has he spoken as pope?

Unlike Paul VI, John Paul II has twice used a formulation that comes close to being a quote of the troublesome statement from the 1971 Synod. However, in each case he has declined to use the word "constitutive." What do the changes indicate? In his address to the Conference of Latin American Bishops at Puebla, Mexico in 1979, he said: "The Church has learned . . . that her evangelizing mission has, as an indispensable part, action for justice and the tasks of the advancement of man."⁹ The available English translations of the Pope's Spanish address have him use Paul VI's word, essential, but in fact he did not. He said *indispensable* not *esencial*. In his address to the Jesuit Provincials summoned to Rome on the appointment of Fr. Dezza as John Paul II's delegate to run the Society (1981), he used the term "integral part."[10] One should note also that most recently, in his address to the delegates to the 33rd General Congregation of the Society (September 1983), he spoke of "the necessity that is found within the evangelizing action of the Church to promote the justice connected with world peace."[11]

Where does the story stand at this point? The Catholic Church continues to struggle over the issue of the Gospel and human liberation. On the one hand, there is no question that a significant development has gained a foothold in the authoritative tradition that could be of immense significance. Whether the word "constitutive" is ever heard again, even if one grants that it needed to be "clarified," the clarification grants more than it rejects. If the very reason for the Church is evangelization, and evangelization involves as an essential (or even just an "integral" or "indispensable") part, "action on behalf of justice," then action on behalf of justice is seen as part of the task of the Church. Nevertheless, the concrete character of Latin American developments clearly continues to vex Church authorities. And so the process of "reception" of the teaching of the 1971 Synod continues. Is action on behalf of the poor essential to the mission of the Church or merely a consequence of its essential mission? Has John Paul II changed his earlier opinion? At this point the Church awaits the comprehensive treatment of liberation theology promised in 1984 by Cardinal Joseph Ratzingher, prefect of the Congregation for the Faith. In the meantime we have the Congregation's "Instruction on Certain Aspects of the 'Theology of Liberation.'" The opening paragraphs hint that the linkage of faith and justice continues to be a subject of concern:

> The Gospel of Jesus Christ is a message of freedom and a force for liberation. In recent years this essential truth has become the object of reflection for theologians, with a new kind of attention which is itself full of promise.
> Liberation is first and foremost liberation from the radical slavery of sin. Its end and its goal is the freedom of the children of God, which is the gift of grace. As a logical consequence, it calls for freedom from many different kinds of slavery in the cultural, economic, social and political spheres, all of which derive ultimately from sin and so often prevent people from living in a manner befitting their dignity. To discern clearly what is fundamental to this issue and what is a by-product of it is an indispensable condition for any theological reflection on liberation.[12]

One must ask: would Paul VI have called liberation from many different kinds of slavery a "logical consequence" of liberation from sin or an "essential part" of that process? Would he have distinguished what is "fundamental" and what is a "by-product" or seen God's saving action as a single integral movement encountering people in all of their relationships?

The not rare reaction to such questions is: what difference does it make? A full discussion of that question would be another paper. I content myself here with pointing out that the Second Vatican Council, which made this whole development possible, was precisely a process whereby the magisterium weighed and absorbed an up-to-then alien theological current (in that case, Northern European theology). Furthermore, the same process engaged in by the Latin American bishops at Medellin was the single most important factor in launching new hopes among the poor of Latin America. In these cases what the magisterium has said has made a difference. More importantly, the reality is that the magisterium of the poor reflects the uncertainty of the institutional magisterium, and so does the nature of their hopes. Thus, in the same *favela* in Brazil we have different perceptions and hopes:

> Claudia: I don't have anything against the Church. But I don't have anything in its favor, either. There's only one God. You don't need churches or *macumba* cults to have faith in God. I talk over all my problems with God. Sometimes I lay down at night and talk with God. I always have that thread of hope that he gives me.
>
> Beti: There comes a time when the poor even curse God, believing that they are praying. "Oh, my God!" But I think that God doesn't want us living in a place like this. He doesn't want us to shut up about things. He wants us to struggle for something. People have this right to struggle. God doesn't want anyone to turn into a beggar. Because if he wanted people to be beggars, he wouldn't have expelled those people who were selling things in the temple.
>
> A long time ago the Church was very aloof from us. Because the Church was dominated by the master, by those who had power. So the Church stood between the rich landowner, and the slave and the Indian, on this side. So it had to stay more on the side of the rich landowner. If the Church had helped only the blacks and the Indians, it would have been persecuted like we were. But nowadays I see the Church defending the *favelado* (slum dweller), discussing the problems of housemaids and workers. The priest stands up to help us who are from the hillsides, from the *favela*, to get together in groups.
>
> A long time ago the Church said that only prayer could save you. Today we know that you have to pray, that you have to trust in

something and ask God for strength to be able to struggle, over-come, speak up, cry out, face problems.[13]

The question at this point could be put: when Beti meets Claudia at the communal laundry, to what extent would the Catholic Church stand behind what she says?

Notes

[1]*We Hold These Truths: Catholic Reflections on the American Proposition* (New York: Sheed and Ward, 1960), pp. 175-196.

[2]"Justice in the World," in *Renewing the Earth: Catholic Documents on Peace, Justice and Liberation*, eds. David J. O'Brien and Thomas A. Shannon (New York: Image Books, 1977), p. 391.

[3]*Theological Studies*, 44 No. 2 (1983), 298-311.

[4]*Ibid.*, p. 301.

[5]*Avvenire*, [Rome] 18 September 1974, p. 1.

[6]C. Caprile, ed., *Karol Wojtyla e il Sinodo dei Vescovi* (Rome, 1980), p. 207.

[7]*Ibid.*, p. 108.

[8]*Evangelii Nuntiandi* (Rome: Vatican City, 1975), paragraph #24. All further references to this work appear in the text.

[9]*Origins*, 8, No. 34 (1979), 35.

[10]*Origins*, 11, No. 39 (1982), 624-628.

[11]*Origins*, 13, No. 14 (1983), 235.

[12]*Origins*, 14, No. 13 (1984), 193.

[13]*Latin American Press*, 18, No. 18 (1985), 3.

CONTRIBUTORS

KENNETH ARROW is the Joan Kennedy Professor of Economics and professor of operations and research at Stanford University. He is the winner of the 1972 Nobel Prize in economics. In 1984 he became the first person outside of Japan to receive the Second Class order of the Rising Sun, the highest honor that nation can bestow on anyone ranking less than a head of state.

A graduate of City College in New York, Arrow received his Ph.D. from Columbia University. He has taught at the University of Chicago, Harvard University and at the Massachusetts Institute of Technology. Arrow has published more than 150 articles in professional journals and is the author of *Social Choice and Individual Values* (1970) and *The Limits of Organization* (1974).

JULIAN BOND first became prominent during the Southern civil rights movements of the 60s. He served four terms in Georgia's House of Representatives, then was elected to the state senate in 1974, where he now serves.

While still a student at Atlanta's Morehouse College, Bond helped found the Committee on Appeal for Human Rights, and the Student Nonviolent Coordinating Committee. At the 1968 Democratic National Convention in Chicago, he became the first black to be nominated for vice president, but withdrew because his age (28 at the time) disqualified him for the post.

Bond serves on several national boards such as the Martin Luther King Jr. Center for Social Change and the Center for Community Change. He is board chairperson of the Southern Elections Fund and President of the Southern Poverty Law Center.

His collected speeches have been published under the title *A Time to Speak, A Time to Act* (1971). His poems and articles have appeared in *Negro Digest, Rights and Reviews, Life, Freedomways, Beyond the Blues, New Negro Poets, American Negro Poets*.

ROBERT MCAFEE BROWN, professor of theology and ethics at the Pacific School of Religion in Berkeley, is author of several books including, *Making Peace in the Global Village* (1981), *Theology in a New Key*) (*1978, Frontiers for the Church Today* (1973), *Religion and Violence* (1973), and *The Ecumenical Revolution* (1967), all of which won the first Sacred Heart Triennial Award for Ecumenical Literature. Brown's most recent book is *Elie Wiesel: Messenger to All Humanity* (1981).

A 1941 graduate of Amherst, Brown earned a bachelor's degree in divinity at the Union Theological Seminary, then took his Ph.D. at Columbia University in 1951.

Before joining the faculty of the Pacific School of Religion in 1979, Brown served as a professor of ecumenics and world Christianity at Union Theological Seminary from 1976 to 1979. From 1962 to 1979 he was professor of religious studies at Stanford University.

CESAR CHAVEZ, president of the United Farm Workers of America, AFL-CIO, founded and leads the first successful farm worker's union in U.S. history.

Born near Yuma, Arizona, César Chávez came from a migrant farm worker family. Growing up in farm labor camps, his education was sporadic. Chávez was forced to quit school in eighth grade to work as a migrant farm worker.

In the late 50s and 60s, Chávez served as national director for the Community Service Organization (CSO). In 1962 he founded the National Farm Workers Association (NFWA).

As a leader, Chávez adheres to the principles of nonviolence. The strike, according to Chávez, is part of a broad movement for social justice and human dignity.

MICHAEL HARRINGTON, co-chair of the Democratic Socialists of America, is the author of *The Other America* (1971), *The Twilight of Capitalism* (1977), *The Politics at God's Funeral* (1984) and, most recently, *The New American Poverty* (1984). He was chair of the Socialist Party of the United States from 1968 to 1972.

Harrington received an A.B. from Holy Cross College in 1947. He attended Yale Law School from 1947-48, received his master's degree at the University of Chicago in 1949 and his Ph.D. at Bard College in 1966.

He has long been active in liberal and trade union causes, serving as a member of Dr. Martin Luther King Jr.'s advisory committee in the 1960s. He has been an active participant in liberal Democratic Party campaigns from 1968 to the present; he served twice as a delegate to Democratic Conventions.

FRANCES MOORE LAPPE, who co-founded the Institute for Food and Development Policy, first gained worldwide attention with the publication of her now classic, *Diet for a Small Planet* (1971), which has sold more than two million copies throughout the U.S., Japan, Germany, France, Sweden and Spain. Lappé is a leading spokesperson for growing numbers of individuals and organizations concerned about world hunger.

Lappé earned a B.A. in history at Earlman College in 1966 and later attended the Martin Luther King School for Social Change and the Graduate School for Social Work at the University of California at Berkeley.

In addition to writing several articles on the topic of world hunger for national publications, such as *Harper's*, *The Nation*, and *The New York Times*, Lappé has co-authored several books with Joseph Collins: *Food First: Beyond the Myth of Scarcity* (1979), *World Hunger: Ten Myths* (1979), *Now We Can Speak: A Journey Through the New Nicaragua* (1982), and *What Difference Could a Revolution Make? Food and Farming in the New Nicaragua* (1985).

ONORA O'NEILL, a native of Northern Ireland, is professor of philosophy at the University of Essex in England, where she served as chairperson of the philosophy department from 1979 to 1982. She was Fagothy Professor of Philosophy for 1984-85 at Santa Clara University. She is author of the soon-to-be-published *Reflections on Famine* and was co-editor of *Having Children: Philosophical and Legal Reflections on Parenthood* (1979).

A 1962 honors graduate of Somerville College at Oxford, where she studied philosophy, psychology and physiology, O'Neill took her Ph.D. in 1968 at Harvard University.

Before joining the University of Essex in 1977, she served as an associate professor at Columbia University, and taught earlier at Wesleyan University in Connecticut.

SHARON N. SKOG, information services director at the Institute for Information Management in Sunnyvale, California, is highly active in state and local Democratic politics. In 1984, Skog served on the Lieutenant Governor's Task Force on Feminization of Poverty, and has been appointed to serve through 1989 as a public member of the California Post-secondary Education Commission.

Skog earned her master's and Ph.D. degrees in political science at the University of California, Santa Barbara. She was an assistant professor of political science at Carroll College in Waukesha, Wisconsin from 1976-1980.

Named one of the Outstanding Young Women of America in 1978, Skog was president of the Palo Alto Democratic Association in 1983-84. She is a member of the Women's Task Force and Women's Political Caucus of the California Democratic Party and also is a member of the National Women's Political Caucus and the Bay Area Women in Political Science.

FRANCIS R. SMITH, S.J. is an assistant professor of religious studies at Santa Clara University. He received his B.S. degree from Santa Clara University in 1956, and his M.A. from Gonzaga University in 1966. In 1976 he took his doctorate in fundamental theology from the Gregorian University in Rome.

His contribution to this volume is one of a series of essays he has written which trace the continuing story of the dialogue between liberation theology and official Roman Catholic teaching. He is currently writing a book entitled *Introduction to Catholic Theology*.

PAUL STEIDL-MEIER is author of *Social Justice Ministry: Foundations and Concerns* (1984), and *The Paradox of Poverty: A Reappraisal of Economic Development Policy*. He teaches at the School of Management at the State University of New York, Binghamton. In 1985, Steidl-Meier was Cassasa Professor of Social Ethics at Loyola-Marymount University.

A research assistant at the Woodstock Theological Center at Georgetown University during 1983-84, Steidl-Meier has focused his studies on social ethics as well as international hunger and rural development. He holds a Ph.D. in economics from Stanford and earned master's degrees in theology at Harvard Divinity School in divinity, at Berkeley's Jesuit School of Theology, and in Philosophy at Gonzaga University in Spokane.

MANUEL VELASQUEZ is director of the Center for Applied Ethics and associate professor of philosophy at Santa Clara University. He received a bachelor's and a master's degree in philosophy from Gonzaga University in 1967 and 1968 respectively. He finished his doctorate in philosophy at the University of California, Berkeley, in 1975. His primary interest is in business ethics, and in 1982 he published a widely-used textbook on the subject, *Business Ethics: Concepts and Cases*. He also co-edited with Cynthia Rostankowski a text with readings on contemporary moral issues. Among his articles on business ethics are: "Ethics in Organizations" in *New Catholic World* (1980); "The Ethics of Organizational Politics" (with G. Cavanagh and D. Moberg) in *Academy of Management Review* (1981); "Teaching Business Ethics: Aims and Methods" in *Doing Ethics in Business*, edited by D. Jones (1982); and "Why Corporations Are Not Morally Responsible for Anything They Do" in *Business and Professional Ethics Journal* (1983). He has also written on the morality of nuclear war and on the socio-economic teaching of the Catholic Church.

WILLIAM WOOD, S.J., executive director of the California Catholic Conference (CCC), is advisor and public policy spokesman for bishops of twelve dioceses.

Before assuming his current post, Wood served as Provincial for Education from 1979-1984 in the California Province of the Society of Jesus. From 1977-1979, he was rector and president of Bellarmine College Preparatory in San Jose. During his tenure at Bellarmine, he founded the Santa Clara Valley Coalition Against Hunger, and the College Park Neighborhood Association.

Wood attended Gonzaga University, Santa Clara University, and Alma College, where he earned master's degrees in philosophy and theology. Later he pursued doctoral studies at the Institute of Spirituality at the Pontifical Gregorian University in Rome.

For the past thirteen years, Wood has focused on the problems of hunger and global poverty as the major aim of his research on faith and justice. He is a member of the California Food Policy Coalition, the Institute for Food and Development Policy, Amnesty International, the Public Concern Foundation, National Conference of Catholic Charities, and National Catholic Education Association.

SELECTED BIBLIOGRAPHY

GENERAL

Beeghley, Leonard. *Living Poorly in America*. New York: Praeger Publishers, 1983.

Boner, Marian O. *General Readings on Poverty: A Selected Bibliography*. Monticello, IL: Vance Biblios, 1970.

Bremner, Robert H. *From the Depths: The Discovery of Poverty in the United States*. New York: New York University Press, 1956.

Chalfant, H. Paul. *Sociological Aspects of Poverty: A Bibliography*. Monticello, IL: Vance Biblios, 1980.

————. *Sociology of Poverty in the United States: An Annotated Bibliography*. Westport, CT: Greenwood Press, 1985.

Dugan, Dennis J. and William H. Leahy, eds. *Perspectives on Poverty*. New York: Praeger Publishers, 1973.

Eames, Edwin and Judith Granich Goods. *Urban Poverty in a Cross Cultural Context*. New York: Free Press, 1973.

Feagans, Lynne and Dale Clark Farran. *The Language of Children Reared in Poverty: Implications for Evaluation and Intervention*. New York: Academic Press, 1982.

Fitchen, Janet M. *Poverty in Rural America: A Case Study*. Boulder, CO: Westview Press, 1981.

Harrington, Michael. *The New American Poverty*. New York: Penguin Books, 1985.

————. *The Vast Majority: A Journey to the World's Poor*. New York: Simon and Schuster, 1977.

Gordon, Margaret S. *Poverty in America*. New York: Irvington Publishers, 1965.

Liftman, Michael. *Power for the Poor: An Experiment in Self Help*. Winchester, MA: Allen & Unwin, Inc., 1978.

Lipton, Michael. *Why Poor People Stay Poor: Urban Bias in World Development*. Cambridge: Harvard University Press, 1977.

Mishra, Ramesh. *The Welfare State in Crisis: Social Thought and Social Change*. New York: St. Martins Press, 1984.

Myrdal, Gunnar. *Challenge of World Poverty*. New York: Random House, Inc., 1971.

Patterson, James T. *America's Struggle Against Poverty*. Cambridge, MA: Harvard University Press, 1981.

Segalman, Ralph and Asoke Basu. *Poverty in America: The Welfare Dilemma*. Westport, CT: Greenwood Press, 1981.

Shaull, Richard. *Heralds of a New Reformation: The Poor of South and North America*. Maryknoll, New York: Orbis Books, 1984.

Stewart, John. *Of No Fixed Abode: Vagrancy and the Welfare State*. Manchester, England: Manchester University Press, 1975.

Streeten, Paul. *First Things First: Meeting Basic Human Needs*. New York: Oxford University Press, 1982.

Valentine, Charles A. *Culture and Poverty; Critique and Counter Proposals*. Chicago: University of Chicago Press, 1972.

Waxman, Chaim Isaac. *The Stigma of Poverty: A Critique of Poverty Theories and Policies*. New York: Pergamon Press, 1977.

Williams, Terry and William Kornblum. *Growing Up Poor*. Lexington, MA: Lexington Books, 1985.

ECONOMIC AND SOCIETAL PERSPECTIVES

Ayers, Robert L. *Banking on the Poor: The World Bank and World Poverty*. Cambridge, MA: MIT Press, 1983.

Coppedge, Robert and Davis, Carlton G. *Rural Poverty and the Policy Crisis*. Aimes: Iowa State University Press, 1977.

Fitchen, Janet M. *Poverty in Rural America: A Case Study*. Boulder, CO: Westview Press, 1981.

Furniss, Norman and Timothy Tilton. *The Case for the Welfare State: From Social Security to Social Equality*. Bloomington: Indiana University Press, 1977.

Galbraith, John Kenneth. *The Nature of Mass Poverty*. Cambridge, MA: Harvard University Press, 1979.

George, Henry. *Progress and Poverty*. New York: Schalkenbach, 1984.

Gilder, George. *Wealth and Poverty*. New York: Basic Books, Inc., 1981.

Hamilton, David Boyce. *A Primer of the Economics of Poverty*. New York: Random House, Inc., 1968.

Lappé, Francis Moore and Joseph Collins. *World Hunger: Ten Myths*. San Francisco, CA: Institute for Food and Development Policy, 1979.

————— . *Food First: Beyond the Myth of Scarcity*. New York: Ballantine Books, 1979.

Levitan, Sar A. and Clifford Johnson. *Beyond the Safety Net: Reviewing the Promise of Opportunity in America*. Cambridge, MA: Ballinger Publishing Co., 1984.

Rodgers, Harrell R. *Poverty Amid Plenty: A Political and Economic Analysis*. Reading, MA: Addison-Wesley Publishing Co., 1979.

Schiller, Bradley R. *The Economics of Poverty and Discrimination*. Englewood Cliffs, NJ: Prentice-Hall, Inc., 1976.

Schiller, John A., ed. *The American Poor*. Minneapolis, MN: Augsburg Publishing House, 1982.

POLITICAL PERSPECTIVES

Barlingay, S.S. *Poverty, Power, Progress*. India: Panchsheel Publishing, 1983.

Bowley, A.L. and M. Hogg. *Has Poverty Diminished?* New York: Garland Publishing, 1985.

Collins, Joseph and Francis Moore Lappé. *What Difference Could a Revolution Make? Food and Farming in the New Nicaragua*. San Francisco, CA: Institute for Food and Development Policy, 1982.

Gauhar, Altaf. *The Rich and the Poor: Development, Negotiations and Cooperation in an Assessment*. Boulder, CO: Westview Press, 1985.

Gronbjerg, Kirsten. *Poverty and Social Change*. Chicago: University of Chicago Press, 1980.

Harrington, Michael. *The Other America*. New York: Penguin Books, 1971.

James, Dorothy. *The Political Science of Poverty and Welfare*. Urbana, IL: Policy Studies, 1974.

King Jr., Martin Luther. *Beyond Vietnam: A Prophecy for the 80's*. New York: Clergy and Laity Concerned, 1982.

MacGregor, Susanne. *The Politics of Poverty*. White Plains, NY: Longman, Inc., 1982.

Murray, Charles. *Losing Ground*. New York: Basic Books, Inc., 1984.

Rein, Mildren. *Dilemmas of Welfare Policy: Why Work Strategies Haven't Worked*. New York: Praeger Publishers, 1982.

Rodgers, Harrell R. Jr. *Poverty Amid Plenty: A Political and Economic Analysis*. New York: Random House, Inc., 1979.

PHILOSOPHICAL AND CULTURAL PERSPECTIVES

Hartman, Robert H., ed. *Poverty and Economic Justice: A Philosophical Approach*. Mahwah, NJ: Paulist Press, 1984.

Plant, Raymond, Harry Lesser and Peter Taylor-Gooby. *Political Philosophy and Social Welfare: Essays on the Normative Basis of Welfare Provision*. London; Boston: Routledge and Kegan Paul, 1980.

Sen, Amartya Kumar. *Poverty and Famines: An Essay on Entitlement and Deprivation*. New York: Oxford University Press, 1981.

THEOLOGICAL AND RELIGIOUS PERSPECTIVES

Nelson, Jack. *Hunger for Justice*. Maryknoll, NY: Orbis Books, 1978.

Paget, Wilkes M. *Poverty, Revolution and the Church*. Greenwood, SC: Attic Press, 1982.

Pilgrim, Walter E. *Good News to the Poor. Wealth & Poverty in Luke-Acts*. Minneapolis, MN: Augsburg Publishing House, 1981.

Sider, Ronald J., ed. *Cry Justice: The Bible on Hunger and Poverty*. New York: Paulist Press, 1980.

Stegemann, Wolfgang. *The Gospel and the Poor*. Philadelphia: Fortress Press, 1984.

VandenBroeck, G. *Less Is More: The Art of Voluntary Poverty*. New York: Harper and Row, 1978.